MATHEMATICAL LITERACY IN THE MIDDLE AND HIGH SCHOOL GRADES

Mathematical Literacy in the Middle and High School Grades

A Modern Approach to Sparking Student Interest

Faith H. Wallace

Mary Anna Evans

With contributions by
Megan Stein

PEARSON

Boston Columbus Indianapolis New York San Francisco Upper Saddle River
Amsterdam Cape Town Dubai London Madrid Milan Munich Paris Montreal Toronto
Delhi Mexico City Sao Paulo Sydney Hong Kong Seoul Singapore Taipei Tokyo

Vice President, Editor-in-Chief: Aurora Martínez Ramos
Associate Sponsoring Editor: Barbara Strickland
Editorial Assistant: Michelle Hochberg
Executive Marketing Manager: Krista Clark
Production Project Manager: Elizabeth Gale Napolitano
Image Permission Coordinator: Mike Lackey
Full-Service Project Management: Pavithra Jayapaul, Jouve India
Manager, Central Design: Jayne Conte
Cover Designer: Bruce Kenselaar
Cover Image: © Frederick Cirou/AltoPress/Newscom
Printer/Binder/Cover Printer: R.R. Donnelley & Sons/Harrisonburg
Text Font: Palatino

Credits and acknowledgments borrowed from other sources and reproduced, with permission, in this textbook appear on pages 147 and 149.

Many of the designations by manufacturers and sellers to distinguish their products are claimed as trademarks. Where those designations appear in this book, and the publisher was aware of a trademark claim, the designations have been printed in initial caps or all caps.

Library of Congress Cataloging-in-Publication Data

Wallace, Faith H.
  Mathematical literacy in the middle and high school grades : a modern approach to sparking student interest / Faith H. Wallace, Mary Anna Evans ; with contributions by Megan Stein.
    p. cm.
  ISBN-13: 978-0-13-218097-9
  ISBN-10: 0-13-218097-9
  1. Mathematics—Studyand teaching (Middle school) 2. Mathematics—Studyand teaching (Secondary) 3. Reading comprehension. 4. Literacy. I. Evans, Mary Anna II. Stein, Megan. III. Title.
QA20.R43W35 2012
510.71′2—dc23

                                                                    2012005793

10 9 8 7 6 5 4 3 2 1

ISBN 10: 0-13-218097-9
ISBN 13: 978-0-13-218097-9

To our teachers . . .

ABOUT THE AUTHORS

Dr. Faith H. Wallace, PhD, is a Professor of Literacy and a reading specialist with a particular research interest in reading in the mathematics classroom. She holds a PhD in language and literacy development, and she has experience as a working middle school teacher of English. The author of a book on reading mathematics, she has written many national peer-reviewed papers for journals including *Action in Teacher Education* and *The Journal of Content Area Reading*. She has also presented at a number of national conferences, including that of the National Council of Teachers of English.

Mary Anna Evans, MS, PE, holds degrees in physics and chemical engineering, and she has classroom experience in math, physics, and chemistry. She is also a novelist, with six books in print. Her writing career took an interesting turn when she learned that teachers were using her mysteries in mathematics classrooms and that publications like *Voice of Youth Advocates* and *School Library Journal* were reviewing them. She has presented at state and national educational conferences, and she has been published along with Dr. Wallace in publications including National Council of Teachers of Mathematics' *Mathematics Teaching in the Middle School* and *Florida Reading Quarterly*.

ABOUT THE CONTRIBUTOR

Megan Stein, BS, studied middle school education at Kennesaw State University, receiving a bachelor's degree with concentrations in math and science. During her studies, Megan earned the Undergraduate Research Award for her work in improving reading literacy through content area academics. She has spoken at several conferences on how to foster reading comprehension and academic performance within the math and science classroom. Megan is also published in National Council of Teachers of Mathematics' *Mathematics Teaching in the Middle School* for her work with content area literacy. She currently teaches eighth grade math and science in an Atlanta-area middle school, giving her up-to-the-minute experience in what works in the classroom and what doesn't. This hands-on expertise has been a valuable adjunct to Faith's expertise in literacy and Mary Anna's science- and technology-based education.

BRIEF CONTENTS

CONTENTS

PREFACE

WHY THIS BOOK AND WHY THESE AUTHORS?

The authors of this book believe that mathematical learning is enhanced by the development of literacy skills. This text will be useful in university education departments to train future classroom teachers in the middle and high school grades. It is also intended to support in-service teachers in their efforts to improve classroom instruction and, as such, would be a valuable resource in middle and high school media centers.

The book in your hands is the result of a chance meeting between two women whose work life trajectories were bound to cross sometime. In other words, their career tracks were certainly not parallel, because they were headed toward the same point.

Dr. Faith H. Wallace is a professor of literacy and a reading specialist with a particular research interest in reading in the mathematics classroom. She is the author of a book on reading mathematics, and she has written a number of peer-reviewed papers and presented at a number of national conferences.

Mary Anna Evans holds a bachelor's degree in engineering physics and a master's degree in chemical engineering. She has classroom experience in math, physics, and chemistry, as well as work experience as an environmental consultant. In training and experience, she is well qualified to address the math-related issues inherent in a book like this. She is also a novelist, with six books in print, and her writing career took an interesting turn when she learned that teachers were using her mysteries in mathematics classrooms. After her first two books, *Artifacts* and *Relics*, were reviewed in *Voice of Youth Advocates* and *School Library Journal*, she found that the mathematics-based and literature-based parts of her career had merged. She began presenting at educational conferences on ways to bring literature into the mathematics classroom, and this is the point at which the nonparallel lines of Faith's and Mary Anna's lives crossed.

The two women met when Mary Anna presented at the National Council of Teachers of English conference, and intellectual sparks flew. They now have more than 5 years of collaboration—papers, presentations, and now this book—in pursuit of a better understanding of how students can become more fluent in mathematics through the use of language.

Megan Stein, whose contributions to this book have been critical to its goal of providing guidance to in-service educators, is a working mathematics teacher, with up-to-the-minute experience in what works in the classroom and what doesn't. This hands-on expertise has been a valuable adjunct to Faith's expertise in literacy and Mary Anna's science-based education.

Faith, Mary Anna, and Megan couldn't be more suited to write this book. They have complementary training and experience, allowing them to view the topic through three different lenses and come up with solutions that couldn't be accomplished through the efforts of one person alone.

HOW TO USE THIS BOOK

This text is divided into three sections designed to make it useful, both as a teaching tool and as a reference. Section I, entitled "Mathematical Literacy" and encompassing Chapters 1 and 2, serves as an overview of our approach to mathematical literacy. Chapter 1 is an exploration of the pervasiveness of mathematics in our language and in our stories. It presents an extended series of examples that discuss the mathematics implicit in a work of popular fiction. These examples can be implemented into the classroom as they are, or they can serve as a model for educators wishing to develop their own. The intent of this chapter is to walk you through the process of unveiling the math in an enjoyable story, so that you can do it for yourself in any text, whether it be the morning newspaper or a blog or the Shakespearean play your students will be reading in their literature course, right after they walk out of your classroom.

Chapter 2 focuses on the pedagogy of mathematics and literacy, based on recent research on reading strategies and vocabulary. It is designed to provide background to educators on what mathematical literacy is and to give them tools for developing it in their students. Sample lesson plans give concrete examples for incorporating these concepts effectively into the middle or high school classroom.

Section II, "Exploring Mathematical Text," includes Chapters 3, 4, and 5. These chapters are intended as a practical resource, giving annotated bibliographies of texts that the authors of this book recommend for the math classroom. Chapter 3 discusses fiction, Chapter 4 discusses nonfiction, and Chapter 5 presents a book form that isn't commonly used in middle and high school grades, the picture book. Sample lesson plans are provided in each of these chapters, giving practical ideas of ways to incorporate these resources into the mathematics classroom.

Section III, "Literacy and Mathematics in Culture," takes the concept of mathematical literacy away from traditional fiction and nonfiction books, moving the focus into the popular culture. The topics presented—poetry, music, environmental print, social media, computer games, reality shows, and more—have the advantage of built-in student interest. To capitalize on this interest, the chapters in this section include suggestions for hands-on classroom activities that are less structured than the formal lesson plans in Sections I and II.

To make the most of this book, learn from the theory presented in Section I, and then explore the resources in Section II and the activities in Section III. This three-pronged approach is designed to jump-start your creativity in the classroom.

ACKNOWLEDGMENTS

We would like to thank the reviewers of this text who provided valuable feedback during the writing process: Amanda L. Glaze, Jacksonville State University; Jeanette Grisham, Northwest Education Service District; Michelle Guy, Jackson Public Schools; Kelly Herman-Roberts, Jones County Schools; Jacy Ippolito, Harvard Graduate School of Education; Jessica Krim, Southern Illinois University Edwardsville; Guyla Ness, Meade School District; Laura Ringwood, Westlake High School; Brooke Trisler, Renton School District; Cathy Williams, San Diego County Office of Education; Mary C. Williams, Still Middle School; and Vicky I. Zygouris-Coe, University of Central Florida.

Section I

Mathematical Literacy

Section I presents an overview of our approach to mathematical literacy, from two very different points of view. Chapter 1 is an informal look at the ways mathematics appears in the language we use to tell our stories, using a work of popular fiction as a vehicle to demonstrate ways to find math where you least expect it. Chapter 2 presents a more academic approach to the following questions: How do we make meaning from symbols, both letter and numbers? How do we help students who are struggling with that meaning-making? The conceptual information in Chapter 1 and 2 will provide necessary background for the hands-on material presented in Sections II and III.

Chapter 1

Exploring the Porous
Boundary Between
Doing Mathematics and
Understanding Text

INTRODUCTION TO MATHEMATICAL LITERACY

In most people's minds, mathematics and reading occupy completely separate territory. Numbers are not letters. Radicals are not commas. The two disciplines don't just use different languages; they use different alphabets.

People are often drawn to one field of study or the other, considering themselves "math people" or "language people." Language people, in particular, often believe that they do not and cannot speak the language of mathematics. It is our position that they are misguided.

While numbers are not letters and radicals are not commas, they are all symbols. They all provide information for readers prepared to decode them. They all derive meaning from the way they are arranged on the page, in sentences and number sentences and paragraphs and proofs.

In this book, we hope to demonstrate ways to teach students to derive mathematics meaning from sources as varied as junk mail, blogs, picture books, and popular fiction. It is critical that students not be allowed to shut themselves off from mathematics by avoiding it. The truth is that they *can't* avoid it. They can certainly choose not to take a course in trigonometry, but they cannot afford to ignore the mathematics implicit in a credit card offer letter. With the information provided in this book, educators will be better equipped to send young people out into the world fully prepared to deal with bait-and-switch interest rates.

We would like to stress that mathematical literacy is not the same as mathematical proficiency. Yes, working math problems is an important part of a mathematics education, and we will be referencing standards, where appropriate, to tie this discussion of math literacy to the practical matter of math proficiency. In particular, we will be referencing the *Common Core State Standards for Mathematics*. Still, our goal is not just to teach students to work problems according to necessarily limited recommendations printed in accepted standards. We would like them to be able to discern the mathematics concealed in the bombardment of text they receive every day. Even more, we would like them to be able to use mathematics to interpret that information in a useful way.

The idea of being proficient in mathematics calls to mind the idea of being able to decipher problems and solve them quickly and correctly. But mathematics and thus mathematical literacy go far beyond practicing problems. They also go beyond being good at a skill set in order to solve classroom textbook activities and arrive at the correct answer—and then start all over again with a new problem.

Instead, students also need to be able to think and communicate in mathematical terms. To be able to code switch between the symbolic systems of language and math is paramount to mathematical literacy. To be able to think and apply mathematical knowledge in real-world situations outside of the traditional problem–solution format is even more important. This aligns with the Common Core standards' stated goal that students must be able to "access the knowledge and skills necessary in their post-school lives" (Common Core State Standards Initiative, 2010).

In a review of research in mathematical literacy, Wallace and Clark (2005) identified three reading stances linked to integrating literacy into the math classroom: Reading Problems, Reading Mathematics, and Reading Life.

The first, Reading Problems, is a standard approach to reading in the math classroom—students read a textbook's instructions to uncover necessary steps to solving a problem, and then they use their mathematical skills to discern an approach to solving the problem quickly and correctly, before moving on to similar problems. This is exemplified in traditional textbooks, which typically use text to explain how a specific type of problem is solved, and then use text again at the beginning of a problem set to give instructions: "Solve each of these equations for x." The student then leaves the world of language and solves twenty similar problems designed to facilitate practice of a single skill. In such situations, arriving at the correct answer is the overriding goal, which can result in missed opportunities to learn from the problem-solving process. Mathematical and reading skills are both exercised, but separately.

The second stance, Reading Mathematics, often involves repeated emphasis on reading problems designed to require students to derive mathematical meaning, bridging the real world with mathematical concepts that might have seemed rote and abstract when limited to problem solving alone. These problems tap into literacy skills, such as decoding text and inferring meaning, that go beyond simply manipulating numbers without understanding why. They require students to integrate language and mathematics, because the problems can't be solved any other way.

While important, the Reading Mathematics stance is still limited. Eventually, students must have the opportunity to read and reason outside the boundaries of problems and solutions. Sometimes there is no right answer. Sometimes there are many. Sometimes only one of those many "right" answers will work in a particular situation. A comprehensive grasp of mathematics can only come when learners recognize that mathematics exists outside the math textbook and that its purpose is to describe their world.

The third and last stance, Reading Life, encourages students to use real-life problems and texts (often called environmental print) to look critically at the intersection between math and everyday life. Plucking examples from the world-at-large gives teachers the opportunity to incorporate a social justice perspective that can be missing from the math classroom (Gutstein, 2006). For example, have you ever read the fine print on a lottery ticket? Do you completely understand the odds of holding a winning ticket? Do you think that lottery tickets are marketed in such a way as to play on the hopes of people who do not have the education to recognize their slim chances of winning?

How about a credit card solicitation? Could a person whose grasp of mathematics is limited to answering structured problems as presented in a textbook be reasonably expected to select the optimum credit card agreement, based on predetermined variables like late fees, transfer fees, and interest rates? Again, is a person who lacks the education to recognize the pitfalls in these agreements at a disadvantage? What about a person who comes from a family whose socioeconomic circumstances made holding a credit card impossible? Would a thorough grounding in mathematical literacy help such a person overcome that disadvantage? The real-world implications of the inability to recognize a bad business deal are a concrete example of the need to promote mathematics as a route to equity for all students.

Our goal in writing this book is to help educators give students a comfort with mathematics that will enable them to tackle these life skills. In the process, we hope that students will also learn to appreciate the elegant equations that describe the twist of a double helix or the vast space between stars, because mathematics explains our universe to us. It is embedded in everything around us. A thorough grounding in mathematics is an ornament to life.

YOUNG CHILDREN LOVE TO COUNT—WHERE DO WE LOSE THEM?

Many students first encounter difficulties in learning math in primary and middle school when trying to derive meaning from a mathematics textbook. This means that teachers working in grades 6 through 12—the target audience of this book—are dealing with young people who have already found themselves flummoxed by the thought of cracking open a math book. The vocabulary is unfamiliar. The pages are laid out differently than in, for example, a history book. There are examples and homework problems and textboxes that define terms and theories and axioms, and these things are presented in a way that can be visually dense—a lot of symbols and equations, accompanied by only a small amount of straightforward text.

When mathematics study progresses from simple arithmetic problems to "word problems" or "story problems," the rubber really hits the road, and that road is the interface between mathematics and language. If you have ever worked a word problem—even a very elementary one like "Johnny has seven apples, but Suzie took one away. Sam gave him three more. It takes six apples to make a pie. Does Johnny have enough to make a pie?"—then you have walked that math/language interface.

Looking at the example word problem about Johnny and his apples, consider the words "took" and "gave." They really don't sound like math words, but in the context of the problem, they tell you to subtract or add in order to get to the answer. Most people, including lifelong math haters, can solve Johnny's apple problem in their heads. The goal of this chapter is to highlight regular words that can signal to readers that a little math is coming their way. Additionally, we want to help you recognize those words, so that you can show your students how to recognize them as well.

ONE TEXT, MANY LESSONS IN MATH LITERACY

This book is an unusual collaboration between a well-credentialed reading specialist and professor of education and an award-winning novelist with a strong background in higher-level mathematics. In later chapters, we will bring in established writers, published in a variety of fields, to give first-person insights that will be useful in using their work in the mathematics classroom.

First, however, we want to examine a substantial passage of fiction in terms of mathematical concepts, and we have the unique opportunity to do this with the work of someone who walks that line between mathematics and language every day of her life—one of this book's co-authors, licensed chemical engineer and novelist Mary Anna Evans.

This will be the first of many times that we explore the intersection between language and vocabulary and mathematics in this book, in keeping with Common Core State Standards for Mathematics, which emphasize the necessity of being able to construct arguments and critique the reasoning of other people (Common Core Standards Initiative, 2010).

As the basis for this discussion, we have created a complete list of the words used in the prologue and first chapter of Ms. Evans' novel, *Artifacts* (2003). The original text of this passage is included in Appendix A for reference, and the word list is included in Appendix B. Throughout the chapter, this word list will serve as a living example of the concepts discussed, and suggestions for classroom discussion and activities will be provided. At the end of the chapter, we have provided a complete lesson plan, referenced to Common Core standards, that might be assigned based on this word list or on other similar lists.

Co-teaching with Computer Educators to Enhance Word Analysis Assignments

Word lists for passages longer than a few paragraphs are very tedious to compile. In order to analyze the long passage from *Artifacts* used in this chapter, the authors made use of an algorithm for creating concordances that required significant manipulation of the text. Involving computer instructors in this project, so that students learn to use the sorting power of word processors, spreadsheets, and database software to quickly prepare word lists for long and complex passages, would be a useful interdisciplinary collaboration. This collaboration is tied to the Common Core standards, which state succinctly to "use appropriate tools strategically" (Common Core Standards Initiative, 2010, p. 7). The labor-intensive process of sorting words is eliminated, and the entire act of creating word lists could be moved out of the math classroom and into the computer technology classroom, saving class time for the more pertinent task of interpreting the mathematics content of the passage being studied.

Artifacts is a mystery featuring an archaeologist, and it was not written with the intent of communicating math skills. It was written for the purpose of telling a good story. Yet mathematics teachers have found lessons in Cartesian coordinates and fractions and simultaneous equations buried in the book that they've been able to use to good effect in their classrooms.

We suggest that, at this point, you take a few minutes to read the text in Appendix A. This will give you a context for the discussion of the mathematics buried in a passage that was written solely to entertain. In all likelihood, the thought of mathematics will not cross your mind while reading.

When you're finished, return to this chapter for an analysis of the ordinal numbers and geometry and other mathematical principles you just absorbed. It is our hope that after you've read the discussion of mathematical language gleaned from this small part of one book, you will find yourself equipped to pluck math concepts out of any book *your* students read and enjoy.

This new skill can serve as the basis of a quick 10-minute activity, such as asking students to silently read a paragraph about adults playing roulette or about children playing a board game, and then asking them to discuss concepts of probability that affect such games. (Hint: A board game played with a spinner will proceed differently than when a player's moves are dictated by a pair of dice. A spinner will give equal odds of giving any number on the dial, whereas the dots on a pair of dice will add up to seven a lot more frequently than they will add up to two or twelve.)

The ability to recognize math in literature can also foster lessons with a greater scope that span the entire curriculum. A math teacher who is teaching a probability unit and who knows that her students are reading Shirley Jackson's *The Lottery* in their literature class can add depth to their experience in both classrooms by comparing the simple lottery in the story to complex state-run lotteries.

But it all starts with being able to look at a story and see the math in it, so go to Appendix A and read a story that's got a lot more math in it than you might think.

Ordinal Numbers, Cardinal Numbers, Numerals, and Other Words Expressing Quantity

We will begin our work with the mathematics in *Artifacts* with one of the most basic concepts in math: quantity. In linguistics, cardinal numbers are words that represent quantity. When   English speaker casually uses the word "number," the meaning generally refers to cardinal numbers—"one," "two," "three," and so on. Ordinal numbers represent the rank of a number in terms of order or position. Examples include "first," "second," and "third." Numerals, symbols that represent quantity like "1," "2," and "3," also appear frequently in fiction, often to represent dates. More general words expressing quantity are very common: "many," "most," and "less" come immediately to mind.

These are words that we all use every day, and the difference between "one" and "1" and "first" is not a difficult concept for most people, so we have chosen this for our first exploration of the list of words in the excerpt from the novel *Artifacts* that is presented in Appendix B.

In reviewing the Common Core standards for the middle and high school grades that are the focus of this book, we found little mention of such a basic element of mathematical understanding as the necessity for building a mathematical vocabulary, beyond general statements like "Make sense of problems and persevere in solving them."

The authors of this book would argue that students need language as a way for their minds to interface with everything in their world, including mathematics. We see the verbal concepts presented in this section, and in this chapter, as rock-bottom fundamentals that must be addressed long before a student tackles algebra or calculus. So bear with us as we start with the words, "one," "two," and "three," and go on from there to build a vocabulary that will interface with any branch of mathematics your students will encounter.

So what numbers did we find in the excerpt from *Artifacts*? Here are the numerals, ordinal numbers, and cardinal numbers we have gleaned from that word list:

> 1, 15, 1782, fifty, first, five, hundred, mid-twentieth, one, second, seventy, ten, thousands, twentieth, two

(Before we continue, does this list make you vaguely uncomfortable? It is presented in alphabetical order, but this bears no resemblance to numerical order. Most people, when looking at this list, will get the sense that something is just . . . wrong. This is an indicator that even people who consider themselves far more oriented toward language than numbers have absorbed mathematical concepts at a subconscious level.)

From an educator's point of view, we should probably first remember that the passage that we have read comes from a mystery novel. When you think about it, this is an awful lot of numbers to be found in a work that isn't about numbers or math. It's simply a story about an archaeologist uncovering a dead body. You will likely find this is true of any written work, after you develop the habit of looking for the presence of math concepts. Such concepts are ubiquitous. People count and measure and plan all the time. There is value in pointing out this fact in the math classroom, and simple exercises like this one are a concrete way to demonstrate the ubiquity of mathematics in daily life.

How might this list be used in the classroom? A quick and easy exercise would be to ask students to look at the list in the previous box and distinguish which words are ordinal numbers, which are cardinal numbers, and which are numerals. A more in-depth exercise would be to ask students to read the source passage silently in class and develop their own lists of such words, which can then be compared to the boxed list in a classroom discussion.

The discussion could turn lively. Students might find themselves returning to the text itself for context, since "second" can be an ordinal number or it can be a unit of time. Which is it in this passage? Context is a powerful thing, in both mathematical systems and language systems. The value of the numeral "2" is very different in the following contexts: 2,000,001 and 1,000,002. And the value of "second" is very different in the following two sentences:

"You only need to stay under water for a second."

"You only need to stay under water for a second minute."

And is "thousands" actually a cardinal number? It doesn't refer to a specific quantity, but could represent any number greater than or equal to two thousand. An advanced student could be set loose on more in-depth reading in linguistics to develop his or her own opinion of whether "thousands" is a cardinal number. The answer to this question is beside the point; the exploration is everything.

Now, let's return to the word list and compile some lists of words that are number related but aren't necessarily ordinal numbers, cardinal numbers, or numerals. Here is a list of some mathematics-related words we compiled from the *Artifacts* word list. Do you agree with the inclusion of some words that are only tangentially related to math, like "a," which communicates something about quantity, and "accompany," which could signal a need for addition if it were encountered in a word problem?

> a, absence, abundance, accompany, all, alone, an, and, another, both, couple, Dernier, each, enough, every, everybody, everyday, everything, exactly, except, few, fraction, gave, get, getting, gift, gifts, given, got, grabbed, half, half-breeds, half-Creek, half-day, including, insufficient, isolation, last, loss, lost, many, missing, more, most, much, nearly, nothing, once, only, plurality, remained, remains, several, some, take, taken

This might be a different list from one that you might compile from the same data source—for example, we have reserved geometry-related words for a later section—but this is a benefit when it comes to fostering classroom discussion.

Notice that some of these words, like "fraction," are clearly math oriented. Some of them, like "gave," are less clearly related, yet they do communicate some sense of quantity. Consider the word problem we discussed in an earlier section:

> Johnny has seven apples, but Suzie took one away. Sam gave him three more. It takes six apples to make a pie. Does Johnny have enough to make a pie?

Most students will recognize, when guided by the teacher, that the word "gave" is a clear indicator that solving this problem will require you to use addition. Giving students the ability to develop a problem-solving strategy based on the verbal description of a real-life problem is the most basic reason for all the activities in this chapter. After a student has dissected the language in the *Artifacts* excerpt and found math there, the task of deciphering a newspaper report on the latest cancer research should be far less daunting.

Looking back at the word list from *Artifacts*, the word "Dernier" isn't even in English, but reading the original passage reveals that "Dernier" is French for "last," which most people would perceive as representing a position in time or numerical order. Notice that context allows us to interpret words in languages that we might not even speak, and it allows us to infer mathematical meaning, as well. At this point, students could be instructed to re-read the passage and state which of those concepts—time or numerical order—was intended by the author when "Dernier" was used in that context.

It's almost inevitable that some readers will perceive mathematical meaning in certain words, while others will disagree. A student who is asked to defend the inclusion of "missing" on her list will be required to draw on verbal, logic, and mathematical skills simultaneously. In other words, she will be asked to dance along that boundary between the verbal world and the numerical world, and that's a good thing.

Geometry—The Shape of Things

Geometry is a branch of mathematics that requires different skills from the math courses that students have taken on their way to the geometry classroom. Geometry requires students to visualize shapes in two or three dimensions. It requires the student to be able to describe an object's position in space. It brings the concepts of measurement and distance into play.

The study of geometry is an opportunity to seize the attention of visually oriented kids who gravitate toward more right-brained activities. It is also an opportunity to teach students with a natural inclination toward math—the kids with a facile understanding of how to push symbols around on a page—what to do when it *isn't* obvious how to solve a problem. First, you draw a picture.

This simple act will often reveal what is known about a problem and what is not known, and how these two factors relate to each other. This may be the most important takeaway skill from the study of geometry, which is so central to the study of math that it is referenced at all levels of the Common Core standards.

So let's look at the word list from *Artifacts* for geometry-related words:

about, above-ground, across, adjacent, against, angle, around, aside, atop, away, balance, base, behind, beneath, beside, between, bottom, broad, by, cavernous, center, crest, crossed, curve, deeper, direction, directions, displaced, distance, down, edge, empty, end, feet, foot, form, formed, forth, fragments, from, front, full, further, gap, grid, here, high, in, inch-long, inch-thick, into, large, largest, left, left-to-right, length, level, lifted, little, long, longer, middle, midst, narrow, next, off, on, onto, open, opened, over, palm-sized, paralleled, part, penetrate, pinpointed, place, point, puny, quarter-inch, radiating, recessed, rectangle, right, ring, row, shape, shaped, size, sizeable, small, solid, somewhere, spiral, spot, spots, square, stick-straight, surface, survey, surveyor's, tall, through, tiny, to, top, topmost, topped, topping, touch, touched, touching, toward, translated, under, underlain, unfolded, up, upper, upward, vertical, west, where, zone

Did you see other spatially oriented words that we missed? This is the beauty of open-ended discussions like those presented in this chapter. One student will get a different answer from a student sitting two seats away. And that's okay.

There are certainly some obvious geometry-related words in the list presented in the previous box: angle, paralleled, point, rectangle, shape, square, translated. Again, it's interesting to find these words in a novel, and this is something you might point out the next time a student asks you, "How are we going to use this in the *real* world?"

(Some things in an educator's life never change. We feel sure that Aristotle asked Plato this age-old question, and then Alexander the Great turned around and asked it of Aristotle. The purpose of this book is to give you some fascinating answers, so that you're ready the next time it pops up.)

What else can we glean from the word list? Many words give a sense of distance: displaced, distance, further, length, long, longer, quarter-inch. Others give an impression of locating an object in two- or three-dimensional space: behind, beneath, between, by, down, front, further, grid, here, inch-long, inch-thick, left, left-to-right, middle, midst, over, right, somewhere, top, topmost, toward, under, underlain, up, upper, upward, west.

Notice how many of these words are prepositions, which are a part of speech that often describes position. "Off the beaten path," "under the boardwalk," and "by the river" are all prepositional phrases that tell the reader where something is . . . and that's geometry.

"Surveyor" and "surveyor's" are of particular interest as geometry-related words, because a land surveyor makes a living through the use of geometrical principles. The notes of two archaeologists who are using the principles of surveying to set up their work site are a critical element of the plot of *Artifacts*, and an important geometric concept—translation—is a clue to the motive for two murders. Was the book written with geometry in mind? Of course not. It was created to entertain people. Can its storyline be used to teach math? Oh, absolutely.

A QUESTION OF TIME

In our culture, children are taught to tell time from an early age, and when we use the phrase "tell time," we don't merely mean understanding the symbols on a clock's face. (Now that most clocks are digital, this is not very complicated.) Implicit in the notion of "telling time" is an understanding of what time means.

If I am brushing my teeth at 7:22 AM, and my school bus comes at 7:30, is this a good thing? A meaningful answer to this question depends on the knowledge of how long it takes me to brush my teeth, whether I can walk right out the door when I'm finished, and how long it takes me to walk to the bus stop. A comprehensive understanding of time as it relates to daily life is one of the most valuable life skills. Chronic tardiness can result in unemployment, which will send the person involved straight to his or her bank account to assess whether there are enough funds in that account to pay the bills. (And bill paying is yet another math skill.)

The concept of time touches every aspect of life, so we would expect our ongoing analysis of the *Artifacts* word list to reveal many references to time, and it does. The list was gleaned from a book centered on archaeology and history, so it is especially rich in such references. It's worth noting that the Common Core standards for middle and high school grades make little mention of time, because concepts related to interpreting time as measured by a clock are taught in the lower grades. Yet Einstein's work in relativity dealt heavily with the concept of time, and the sciences frequently measure physical phenomena in terms of time. Velocity is defined as the distance traveled divided by the time elapsed. The unit of "hertz" expresses cycles per second. It seems appropriate to retain some focus on time in middle and high school grades, as students mature into an ability to comprehend the subtleties of time measurement.

Even beyond the list presented in the following box, an argument could be made that nearly every English verb could be considered time related. Consider the irregular verb, "to be," and some of its derivatives, "was," were," "is," "am," and "been." The verb form communicates very clearly whether the action being discussed takes place in the present or in the past. The form "will be," is one way that this verb can take the reader into the future. Similarly, an action verb like "run" can communicate the passage of time through its various tenses: "run," "ran," and "will run."

Review this word list and consider whether you agree with the words we've chosen to include.

> after, age, already, always, ancient, as, awaited, awhile, before, centuries, century, contemporary, current, date, dated, day, day's, days, decades, early, finally, former, later, minute, moment, now, old, past, paused, primeval, recent, since, sometimes, sudden, time, times, tomorrow, Tuesday-night, when, while, whilst, will, year's, years, yet

What's the Likelihood of Finding Math in Your Pleasure Reading?

Other instances of math in day-to-day life include logic, probability, and finance. Almost everyone who claims a complete mathematical ineptitude can handle pocket change competently. When we pay for purchases in cash and make change, deciding the optimum number of quarters, nickels, dimes, and pennies to complete the transaction, we are doing algebra, whether the math-phobes of the world want to believe it or not. Virtually all of us have some sense of how likely it is that a given lottery ticket is a winner, whether we want to admit it or not. The ability to follow a line of reasoning like this, "If the phone rings and if I take the time to answer it, then I will be late for work," is a clear indication of an understanding of basic logic.

To round out this chapter, we have compiled a list of words for each of these disciplines—logic, probability, and finance. A similar list can be gleaned from almost any passage plucked randomly from a book, magazine, newspaper, or website. Asking students to look for those words in their out-of-class reading and then share examples with the class is a good way to sharpen their observation skills and their understanding of the presence of mathematics in their personal lives.

> *Logic:* if, maybe, no, nor, not, or, sure, surely, then, therefore, unless, whether, which, why
>
> *Probability:* likelihood, likely, probably, rarely, sample, samples, sampling, unlikely
>
> *Finance:* interest, pay, paycheck

LOOKING FOR MATHEMATICAL TEXT IN YOUR STUDENTS' WORLD

Have we completely dissected the possibilities of our *Artifacts* word list yet? No, and that's a beautiful thing. One rewarding activity might be to discuss the mathematical concepts presented earlier and then send students to the original book excerpt and ask whether the narrative itself has a direct link to mathematics.

A long-term assignment might include instructions to read the entire novel, with different students asked to write papers on various mathematical angles that can be teased out of the narrative. For example, a considerable portion of the multiracial protagonist's genealogy can be inferred from the story. Is it possible to estimate the relative proportions of her heritage that originate in Africa, Europe, and the Americas? Another assignment might be a paper describing the methods that surveyors use to measure large areas of land.

Another paper still might stem from the notion of compounded interest, based on a scene late in the book describing the growth of an interest-bearing bank account that was established in the 1960s.

Less open-ended questions appropriate for classroom discussion might include the following:

Classroom Discussion Questions for *Artifacts*

1. When the word "foot" is mentioned, does it refer to the unit of measurement or to the part of Faye's body that is attached to her leg? When the word "second" is used, is Faye focused on the second in a list of objects she's counting, or is she thinking of a unit of time? Can we answer those questions from the list, out of context, or must we return to the original text and read the sentence from which the words came?

2. How does mathematics relate to the work life of a real archaeologist? Is measurement an important part of the profession? Counting? Statistics? Can an archaeologist survive without geometry? (Hint: If you dig up an artifact that turns out to be proof that Martians landed in 20,000 B.C.E., you're going to want to send a work crew back to the spot where you dug it up. It would behoove you to be able to find the spot.)

At the conclusion of this chapter, we have included a complete lesson plan based on a scene from *Artifacts* where the characters are all astonished at the size of an interest-bearing bank account that was established in the 1960s. Our intent is that this plan could serve as a model for developing your own classroom activities from whatever book is setting your students' imaginations aflame. Has this discussion prepared you to pluck mathematics out of other non–mathematics-related books? Do you think that these exercises will help your students learn to do the same thing?

When you think your students are ready to try their wings, take these exercises into new territory, trying assignments like these:

Helping Students Find Math in Unexpected Places

1. Provide a short reading passage of your choice, and ask your students to make their own lists of math-related words. Then ask the students to discuss their lists and defend their word choices.
2. Ask your students to write an essay on any subject, and then surprise them with an assignment to pluck math words out of their own prose. They will likely be shocked to see how naturally their mind handles mathematical concepts.

These projects can be integrated with teachers in other subject areas. Math teachers and English teachers can team up to investigate the mathematics buried in the texts that students are reading for English class. Computer technology teachers can assist with the database aspect of compiling a list of mathematical words from a reading passage.

When these projects are all in the past, your students will have internalized the concept of mathematics as presented in text, and they will carry this concept with them, whether they are reading a mathematics textbook, a business balance sheet, or the sales pitch for a life insurance policy. Their understanding of math will be better integrated with their understanding of verbal communication, and this integration is a good thing to have.

LESSON PLAN 1-1

INTERESTED IN GETTING RICH? AN INVESTIGATION OF SIMPLE INTEREST, COMPOUND INTEREST, AND EXPONENTIAL FUNCTIONS BASED ON *ARTIFACTS*

This lesson plan is designed to give a comprehensive approach to demonstrating that mathematics content can be found anywhere, even in popular fiction. The lesson plan includes guided questions that preteach vocabulary or concepts that will be reinforced and practiced throughout the reading assignment and further activities.

(Continued)

LESSON PLAN 1-1 (Continued)

Materials & Preparation: Worksheet, pencils, graph paper, *Artifacts*, calculators (optional)

Duration: 45–60 minutes or homework assignment

Applicable Common Core Standards:

Grade 6: Ratios and Proportional Relationships

Expression and Equations

Grade 7: Ratios and Proportional Relationships

The Number System

Expressions and Equations

Grade 8: Expressions and Equations

Geometry

High School:

Algebra: Seeing Structure in Expressions

Reasoning with Equations and Inequalities

Functions: Interpreting Functions

Linear, Quadratic, and Exponential Models

Modeling

Procedure: Spark students' interest by shouting phrases like, "No interest until January!" or "Buy now and get a special reduced interest rate!" in the same fashion that they have likely heard on radio and television commercials. Ask students for examples of times when they have heard the words "interest" and "rate" in advertisements, and then ask them to explain the concept of interest from the point of view of the consumer.

After a short discussion activating prior knowledge of the financial concepts of interest paid to individuals who have invested money and interest paid by individuals who have borrowed money, hand out the prereading questions. These questions will expose students to the interest formula, its variables, and how to find various information depending on what variables are defined. You may instruct students to work independently or in groups depending on ability level and strength in prerequisite skills, like solving multivariable equations. After allowing students time to discuss and work the problems, you may choose to have a short lesson or discussion to clear up any misconceptions about appreciation, interest, and rate.

Assign the excerpts from *Artifacts* and the postreading activity sheet for students to complete as they read. As students work through the plot of the story, they will uncover mathematical vocabulary related to the material taught in the prereading activity. Students can continue practicing and extend their knowledge of interest with the real-world scenarios discussed in the novel. By the time the students have completed the pre- and postreading activities, they will have a deeper understanding of the content as well as its real-world applications discussed in the novel.

Percentage, Interest, and Appreciation Prereading Questions

1. True or false? Interest is calculated based on the amount of the original investment, also known as the principal.

Answer: True

   Simple annual interest is calculated with the following algebraic formula: $I = P \times R \times T$, where I represents the amount of interest, P is the amount of the principal or original investment, R is the annual interest rate written in the form of a decimal, and T is the time in years that the money is invested.

   For example, the interest on $50 invested at a 6% annual rate for a year is $50 \times 0.06 \times 1$, or $3. To get the total amount of the investment at the end of the year, add the principal and the amount of interest earned, which would yield $53 for this problem.

   Try this problem on your own: Sara invested $100 for 1 year. At the end of that year, she received $109. What annual rate of simple interest did she receive?

   a. 0.09%

   b. 0.90%

   c. 9% – Correct answer. Interest of $9 equals Principle ($100) × Rate × Time (1 year). Solving the equation yields a rate of 9%.

   d. 90%

2. Appreciation is found by subtracting the original value of an asset from its appreciated value. For example, a piece of land that was bought for $10,000 and sold for $25,000 has appreciated by $15,000.

   Try this problem on your own: A house was purchased in 1989 for $175,000. It was sold in 2004 for $235,000. What was the total amount of appreciation?

Answer: $235,000 − $175,000 = $60,000

Reading Passages

Excerpt from *Artifacts*, pages 58–60

"Thank you for taking the time to see me," Faye began. She didn't want to try [the senator's] patience and she'd never been one to beat around the bush anyway, so she plunged directly to the point. . . .

(Continued)

LESSON PLAN 1-1 (Continued)

"Seagreen Island is mine," she said. "Well, it should be. My great-great-grandfather purchased Last Isle in the 1850s, back when it was all one island. Shortly after he bought it, the great hurricane of 1856 carried away most of the island, along with a few hundred planters and their families and slaves. There was a resort there at the time."

"I've heard the story."

The adrenaline was getting to Faye. . . . "Most people haven't," she said. "If a bunch of rich Astors and Vanderbilts and Roosevelts had been swept off Cape Cod, it would be in the history books."

"There was a war coming on in 1856, and the victors do write the history books." . . . .

"Yeah, but if somebody had bothered to write about what happened on Last Isle," she rattled on, "my great-grandmother might never have lost her land." . . . .

"This dispute is older than I am. Why are you coming to me now?"

"Don't you see? Some of my land has been absorbed into the wildlife refuge. Let them keep it. It's not fair, but at least they're preserving it. Help me get Seagreen Island back . . . and no tacky tourists will ever tear up the place. Your voters will be happy, and God knows that will make you happy."

Excerpt from *Artifacts*, page 98

"Your problem is an interesting and important one," [the senator said]. If your claims prove true, then your family was defrauded of a piece of property whose value has appreciated significantly the past few years."

Excerpt from *Artifacts*, pages 284–285

After everyone drank to Abby, [the sheriff] said, "I guess you folks have heard about the bones that keep washing ashore on Seagreen Island."

"Are they Abby's?"

"Maybe. It'd be hard to prove. . . ."

"Do you have the arm bones? The right upper arm?" Douglass asked. . . . "Because I was there when she broke it . . . . I've got a picture of her in the cast."

"It's circumstantial," the sheriff said. "Reckon it'd be enough to get the trustee of Mr. Williford's estate to release the reward money at this late date?"

"I imagine so," Douglass responded, "considering that I'm the trustee."

Everybody looked at Faye, who didn't want to be crass and ask, "How much?" She stifled the question with a loud exhalation.

"Don't know how much, exactly," Douglass said. "I don't check regularly, because it just sits in the bank and earns interest. The reward was twenty thousand dollars in 1964. Reckon it would make a regular person rich, but you're gonna blow it on this house. Reckon it'll just make you comfortable."

Faye wondered how long it would be before she could breathe again.

Postreading Questions Based on the Excerpts from *Artifacts*

3. You were told in the excerpt that Faye's property on Seagreen Island has appreciated in value significantly. Assume the island—valuable beachfront property—was worth $120,000 in 1856. If it was worth $720,000 when Faye's family was defrauded of it in 1932, how much had it appreciated during that time?

Answer: $720,000—$120,000 = $600,000

4. If the current value of Seagreen Island is $12,000,000, how much has its price appreciated since 1932? And how much has its price appreciated since 1856?

Answer: Since 1932: $12,000,000 − $720,000 = $11,280,000

  Since 1856: $12,000,000 − $120,000 = $11,880,000

5. As we learned in Question 1, simple interest is calculated by applying the interest rate to the original amount invested. Simple interest on $1,000 invested at 10% will be $100 per year. Think about this for a minute. That means, after the first year, there will be a $1,100 in your account, but you will only be earning interest on the original $1,000. You would be much happier if you earned interest on your whole account—$1,100—during the second year, wouldn't you? This is called **compounding**.

• Let's try going further with the idea of compounding. If you earn 10% interest on $1,100 during the second year, how much money will be in your account?

Answer: $1,100 + ($1,100 × 0.10) = $1,210

• If you earn 10% interest again in the third year, how much interest will you earn?

Answer: $1,210 + ($1,210 × 0.10) = $1,331

You can see that calculating compounded interest year by year over a period of 100 years would get very old. Fortunately, there is a formula to calculate compounded interest over any period of time: $A = P(1 + r)^n$, where **A** is the amount of money accumulated at the end of the investment period, **r** is the interest rate expressed as a decimal, and **n** is the number of years in the investment period.

You may use a calculator for this problem:

• Using the formula provided above, calculate the amount of money in an account after 20 years, if the initial deposit was $300 and the interest is 8%, compounded annually.

Answer: $300(1.08)^{20} = $1,398

(*Continued*)

LESSON PLAN 1-1 (Continued)

6. You may use a calculator for this problem.

When Douglass tells Faye that she will receive the $20,000 reward, plus the interest it has earned since 1964, she finds that she is unable to breathe. *Artifacts* was published in 2003, 39 years after the money was invested in 1964. If we assume an average interest rate during those 39 years of 5%, compounded annually, how much money will she receive? Why can't Faye breathe?

Answer: $20,000(1.05)^{39} = $134,095. If Faye was lucky, the interest rate was more than 5%. Invested at 10%, the total would be $822,895. Would you have expected the number to be so big?

Let's hope Douglass invested that money well!

References

Common Core State Standards Initiative. (2010). *Common Core State Standards for English language arts & literacy in history/social studies, science, and technical subjects.* Washington, DC: National Governors Association Center for Best Practices and the Council of Chief State School Officers. 4, 39–84.

Evans, M. (2003). *Artifacts.* Scottsdale, AZ: Poisoned Pen Press. 1-16, 58-60, 98, 284–285.

Gutstein, E. (2006). *Reading and writing the world with mathematics: Toward a pedagogy for social justice.* New York: Routledge.

Wallace, F. H., & Clark, K.K. (2005). Reading stances in mathematics: Positioning students and texts. *Action in Teacher Education, 27*(2), 68–79.

Chapter 2

Reading Strategies:
Making Meaning of
Mathematical Text

INTRODUCTION

Supporting student reading isn't such a difficult task when we remember that reading is about making meaning—about being strategic in approaching text that is difficult to understand at first glance. When students are asked what to do when they are trying to read something they don't understand, students of all ages will often immediately say something like, "Sound it out." In other words, they are describing the strategy they use to decode a word they don't recognize. But what should readers do when they encounter an entire passage that doesn't make sense to them?

Reading is an active process (Goodman, 1996); readers have to work to make meaning, by making connections, asking questions, and visualizing what they are reading (Harvey & Goudvis, 2000). Effective readers monitor their comprehension and know when they need to make adjustments (Rhodes & Shanklin, 1993). How many times have you gotten to the bottom of a page and realized you had no idea of what you read? What did you do? Go back?

Struggling readers don't always realize that reading is supposed to make meaning, and when they realize that they don't understand what they just read, they often simply keep going, because they think that reading is just about decoding the words. Teaching students to monitor their comprehension can help them to be more strategic readers.

HOW DOES READING MATHEMATICS DIFFER FROM OTHER KINDS OF READING?

Historically, most reading done in the mathematics classroom involves technical prose, such as in a textbook (Alvermann & Moore, 1991). Reading a textbook is different from reading other types of texts, posing specific obstacles to making meaning (Koebler & Grouws, 1992).

In writing this chapter, we reviewed a textbook currently in use for a sixth-grade mathematics course. We opened the book randomly, finding a two-page layout on variables and expressions. The concepts presented on those two pages included variables, constants, and algebraic expressions. The procedure for evaluating algebraic expressions with one missing variable was presented, followed by the procedure for evaluating algebraic expressions with two missing variables. Students were also instructed in methods for translating between symbols of multiplication and division. Even for an adult experienced in mathematical concepts and procedures, this is a lot of material for two pages.

On the two pages following that two-page layout, students were given guided practice, independent practice, and standardized testing preparation questions. There were over thirty questions with several multistep problems that required students to use skills that included completing tables and reading graphs. This density of text is necessary when the volume of material presented in a year-long mathematics class is considered, but it is difficult for anyone to read and interpret. Simply looking at all those numbers, letters, and symbols is daunting enough to make a struggling reader want to close the book.

How can we help that struggling reader?

Because of the volume of material that must be presented, chapters must include many new terms and concepts in a short amount of space, which requires very complex text structures. For example, students are often conditioned to find the topic sentence at the beginning of a paragraph, but in a math textbook, the topic sentence may be in the middle or at the end of the paragraph, after several supporting statements, a newly defined word, and a formula that consists of three letters, four numbers, and two symbols.

Mathematics textbooks often present new ideas multimodally, where words, symbols, and abbreviations are all used to represent words and concepts. Words can have multiple meanings and can represent concepts, operations, or relationships, which adds yet another meaning-making layer. A still more confusing phenomenon is the redefining of sight words the student already knows, giving them new mathematical meanings that bear little resemblance to familiar concepts (Hancewicz, Heuer, Metsisto, & Tuttle, 2005; Hiebert et al., 2003; Smith, 2002).

For example, consider these words:

point

model

formula

mean

set

Taken out of context, even a math teacher might hesitate when asked what they mean (and even the word "mean" can have a different meaning for mathematicians than for others). An adult might know that babies drink something called "formula" because the manufacturers have historically promoted it as being mixed according to a formula that was designed to make sure that nutrients were available in the proportions most conducive to health. But do adolescent students have this prior knowledge? The following concatenation of numbers and letters looks nothing like the white powder that parents mix with water to feed their infants:

$$a^2 + b^2 = c^2$$

Similarly, anyone who thoroughly grasps what a mathematician means by the words "set," "model," and "point" could explain the relationships between the mathematical concepts and the colloquial uses of the words. But a middle schooler who has only encountered these words in casual conversation is likely to be flummoxed, particularly if that middle schooler's vocabulary skills aren't strong in general. It's important for a math teacher to remember to take time when teaching new material, early on, to teach the vocabulary that is specific to mathematics.

If reading a math textbook poses such problems, why would we even suggest adding reading material to a math classroom? We suggest it because a carefully selected novel or trade nonfiction book can tie the abstract world of mathematics to the world that students inhabit and understand. It can give them the prior knowledge to know that "modeling" does not necessarily mean posing for pictures. It can bring the theoretical world to life.

HOW CAN WE HELP STUDENTS MAKE MEANING FROM MATHEMATICAL TEXT?

The meaning of a word, paragraph, chapter, or book is inextricably linked to the reader's prior knowledge of the material being presented. Even a chunk of text as simple as this—C-A-T—is meaningless if you've never seen a cat or if you don't speak English.

This prior knowledge, sometimes referred to by the term "schema" (Alvermann, Phelps, & Gillis, 2010; Goodman, 1996), allows the reader to easily access related information, assimilate new information, determine the importance of new information, and much more. Making meaning from a math textbook that is full of information for which the reader has little or no prior knowledge is an opportunity for failure.

Television producers show awareness of the importance of prior knowledge when a show opens with scenes reviewing the action in previous shows. Otherwise, viewers who missed a show or, worse, have never seen an episode of that program can be left behind.

In a more complex example, imagine yourself watching a trailer for a movie. There are random scenes of exciting events—explosions, helicopter crashes, beautiful people running for their lives—but no information that can help you piece together the plot. And then the image of something specific and familiar, maybe the theft of a unique artwork, triggers a memory, and you have a little a-ha moment. You realize that you have read the book on which this movie is based, and now everything makes sense.

A common metaphor for the storage and access of knowledge in the brain is the filing cabinet model—this is how one of this book's authors, Dr. Faith Wallace, was first introduced to the concept of prior knowledge. She remembers viewing a transparency of the brain with a file cabinet over it, which imagines the brain as a grouping of file folders where information is stored. These folders are labeled in such a way as to facilitate information retrieval, and then they themselves are stored in drawers and cabinets, which are also organized by topic.

Perhaps a better metaphor for the current generation is to think of the brain as being similar to the Internet. Information is accessed through connections that are much like hyperlinks linking far-flung storage devices. Using this model, it is reasonable to think of prior knowledge as being the search engine that helps us navigate those links. When you "type" a C and an A into your prior knowledge search engine, it begins offering you options, just as your Internet search engine does, asking you whether you're looking for "cat" or "California" or "catastrophe." Without the help of that prior knowledge, you would spend a lot more time sifting through your knowledge and memory for the tidbit of information you're seeking.

Relating this model of the brain to reading and meaning making, the speed with which you get to the meaning of something you are reading just might have to do with how much prior knowledge you have about the topic. How quickly can you relate new material to something you already understand?

Classroom time is, by necessity, dedicated both to storing new information in the databases between your students' ears and to building links that will help them find that information later, when they need it. This is the knowledge base that they will take with them when they leave your classroom. And perhaps the day will come when one of your students is mixing powdered formula for his baby's bottle and the hyperlink between his world and the things he learned in your math class lights up.

"So *that's* why they call this stuff formula!"

Prior Knowledge: An Experiment

Read the following passage and be prepared to answer some questions about its content:

So this was Excellent? Lots of traps on this one, I thought as I walked. From the line I saw the tunnel to the triple and the weave to the see-saw – talk about discrimination! Maybe I will lead out. Planning ahead, I would probably have to pivot or flip to get to the table. After that maybe a front cross to the double and rear cross to the walk? That serpentine will cause problems getting her to scramble. Better hit my contact—running or target? I think this should be easier since we are at 20 now—Preferred. No MACH in our future no matter what happens today, but at least we can double Q.

Now, what do you think this passage is about? Did reading this passage give you some degree of sympathy for students from different cultures who try to make sense of the proceedings in an American classroom, especially students who are not native English speakers?

Were you able to read to decode the passage and make meaning? Or were you left scratching your head wondering what that was about?

For fun, one of this book's authors, Dr. Faith Wallace, wrote this passage and gave it to the other author, Mary Anna Evans, and asked Mary Anna to tell her what it meant. Here are some quotes from Mary Anna's response:

"Maybe it was about something to do with flying – a MACH is referenced and other military words like contact, pivot, and flip."

"By the capitalization of Excellent, I infer that the narrator is looking at something that can be named, possibly a place."

"There is a military or paramilitary sound to much of the language, and I'm guessing that this passage comes from a science fiction or military fiction work."

Please know that, even though Mary Anna had no idea what Faith was writing about, she was still using some degree of prior knowledge, because she knows that Faith reads a great deal of science fiction. What she forgot, however, is that Faith also trains dogs for agility trials. The passage is written from the point of view of a trainer preparing to begin a competition.

Faith also tested her premise in the classroom, asking students to interpret the passage. When asked what activity the narrator was describing, she got guesses that ranged from gymnastics to video gaming to snowboarding. None of the students was able to define "scramble" in the context of the passage, yet nearly all the students were able to infer that "20" and "Preferred" had the same meaning, based on the second to last sentence.

So what would it have taken to give students the prior knowledge needed to understand the passage? A crash course in dog agility? No. It could have been done with nothing more than a quick viewing of a 1-minute video of a dog running an agility course, with narration that points out that when the dog runs up and over an A-frame–shaped obstacle, she is "scrambling."

Before giving any reading assignment, it is essential to consider whether students' prior knowledge is sufficient for them to understand it. Questions designed to test understanding must be carefully framed. Remember that Faith's students were able to infer the meaning of "Preferred" without ever understanding what the passage was really about. But without a careful assessment of the reading assignment before it is given and, if necessary, a prereading discussion of unfamiliar concepts and vocabulary that will be encountered in the passage, any class time spent reading can be utterly wasted.

Helping students with meaning making starts early, long before they encounter the text they will be reading. Your care in choosing and evaluating any text to be read in the classroom will be inherent in any later use of that text. For this reason, it is essential not to rely on a book review, or even on the recommendations in this book. You must read material to be assigned personally, in order to assess appropriateness for *your* students. Nobody knows your readers better than you.

While reading, think about where your students might struggle, focusing on text structure, vocabulary, and prior knowledge. Are there too many new vocabulary words? Is the sentence structure confusing?

Then develop lesson plans with this evaluation in mind. Do you need to preteach math concepts or vocabulary on which this new text builds?

USING READING ACTIVITIES TO ENHANCE STUDENT UNDERSTANDING

Before beginning reading, students benefit by being reminded of their goals, and those goals aren't always the same. Most reading material can be read with one of the following three goals in mind (Wallace, Clark, & Cherry, 2006):

How come?

What if?

So what?

Nonfiction text is often read with the motivation to find out facts—in other words, to answer the question, "How come?" Fiction explores imaginary worlds that are rife with the possibilities implicit in the question, "What if?" And the special type of text called "environmental print"—the barrage of text that flows into our lives through sources like the Internet, the mailbox, billboards, and instruction manuals—typically addresses the question of "So what?" We have included an entire chapter devoted to each of these types of reading material in this book (Chapters 3 through 8) to help you explore those questions with your students.

Among the structured activities presented in the academic literature that pertain to the importance of prior knowledge to literacy is the comprehension guide proposed by Harold Herber (1978). A variation on Herber's comprehension guide, the Three-Level Comprehension Guide described by Alvermann et al. (2010) in *Content Area Reading and Literacy*: *Succeeding in Today's Diverse Classrooms*, is the basis for the example project at the end of this section, based on Lewis Carroll's classic novel, *Alice's Adventures in Wonderland*. Such comprehension guides are excellent tools to help students apply prior knowledge to the texts they read.

At the end of this chapter, we have included three sample lesson plans designed as structured activities used to explore important elements of meaning making, such as prior knowledge, vocabulary, and questioning. First, however, we want to discuss one activity, the comprehension guide to *Alice's Adventures in Wonderland*, within the context of the chapter. It is based on a classic work of fiction familiar to nearly everyone, yet one that is not likely to be the first story one thinks of when one thinks, "mathematics." It is simply and quickly presented, yet it follows Alvermann's Three-Level Comprehension Guide, discussed earlier, by asking three questions aimed at progressive levels of understanding—literal, interpretive, and applied—and it addresses these important concepts from Common Core standards (Common Core State Standards Initiative, 2010).

Common Core Standards:

Grade 6: Expressions and Equations

    Ratios and Proportions

Grade 7: Expressions and Equations

    Ratios and Proportions

    The Number System

Grade 8: Expressions and Equations

    Functions

High School:

Algebra: Reasoning with Equalities and Inequalities

    Modeling

This exercise uses a familiar work of fiction to introduce a less familiar mathematical concept—ratio—and asks the student to continually compare what he or she reads and computes against the prior knowledge that will make it

Reading Guide: *Alice in Wonderland*

Comprehension Guide

Read the following excerpt from *Alice's Adventures in Wonderland* and follow the instructions below:

> This time Alice waited patiently until it chose to speak again. In a minute or two the Caterpillar took the hookah out of its mouth and yawned once or twice, and shook itself. Then it got down off the mushroom, and crawled away in the grass, merely remarking as it went,
>
> "One side will make you grow taller, and the other side will make you grow shorter."
>
> "One side of WHAT? The other side of WHAT?" thought Alice to herself.
>
> "Of the mushroom," said the Caterpillar, just as if she had asked it aloud; and in another moment it was out of sight. . . .
>
> It was so long since she had been anything near the right size, that it felt quite strange at first; but she got used to it in a few minutes, and began talking to herself, as usual. "Come, there's half my plan done now! How puzzling all these changes are! I'm never sure what I'm going to be, from one minute to another! However, I've got back to my right size: the next thing is, to get into that beautiful garden – how IS that to be done, I wonder?" As she said this, she came suddenly upon an open place, with a little house in it about four feet high.
>
> "Whoever lives there," thought Alice, "it'll never do to come upon them THIS size: why, I should frighten them out of their wits!"
>
> So she began nibbling at the righthand bit again, and did not venture to go near the house till she had brought herself down to nine inches high.
>
> (Lewis Carroll, 1916, pp. 28–30)

1. Literal. Place a checkmark next to the statement (or statements) you think says the same thing the author says.
   _____ a. Alice is able to make herself normal-sized after the caterpillar tells her the secret of the mushroom.
   _____ b. The mushroom Alice is carrying has the power to make her larger or smaller.
   _____ c. Alice can control her size by the side of the mushroom she nibbles.

Answer: All of these statements are true, based on Carroll's text.

2. Interpretive. Check the statement (or statements) you think the author implies. Some thinking is required! Be ready to support your answers.
   _____ a. Alice can control her size by the amount of mushroom she eats.
   _____ b. Alice, at normal size, is too big for a house that is 4 feet tall.
   _____ c. Alice's normal size is bigger than 9 inches.

Answer: All of these statements are true, based on Carroll's text.

> Reality check: Using your prior knowledge, think about the size of a house and the size of a little girl. Does it make sense that a normal-sized girl is too big for a 4-foot-tall house? Does it make sense that she is taller than 9 inches?

3. Applied. Answer the following questions
  a. If Alice is 9 inches tall and the house is 4 feet tall, what is the ratio of her height to the height of the house?

Answer: 9:48, or 3:16

  b. If one bite of mushroom always increased Alice's height by 8 inches, can you write an algebraic formula to describe that relationship? Let H represent her new height in inches, let h represent her old height in inches, and let b equal the number of bites taken.

Answer: $H = h + 8b$

  c. If Alice's normal height is 4 feet tall, use the ratio you calculated in question a to calculate the height of a house that is proportionate to the one described in the book.

Answer: $4/x = 3/16$. Solving for x yields 64/3, or 21 1/3 feet

  d. Does this sound like a reasonable height for a house? How tall do you think your house is? How tall are you? What is the ratio of your height to your house's height?

easier to recognize whether the answer obtained from working a math problem is plausible. And did you notice Alice's confusion over the Caterpillar's meaning?

"One side will make you grow taller, and the other side will make you grow shorter."

"One side of WHAT? The other side of WHAT?" thought Alice to herself.

"Of the mushroom," said the Caterpillar, just as if she had asked it aloud . . .

Even in Wonderland—or maybe especially in Wonderland—meaning making can be impossible without the necessary prior knowledge.

LESSON PLAN 2-1

A MIRROR TO NATURE ANTICIPATION GUIDE

In an anticipation guide, questions given before a reading assignment are geared toward preteaching concepts, vocabulary, or opening discussion for further instruction on a concept. Prereading activities are often paired with a postreading activity so that students can practice concepts, revisit their original answers, and possibly form new opinions.

Materials: *A Mirror to Nature* by Jane Yolen, printed Anticipation Guide

Duration: 25 minutes: 5 minutes prereading, 10 minutes reading, and 10 minutes postreading and discussion

(Continued)

LESSON PLAN 2-1 (Continued)

Applicable Common Core Standards:

Grade 7: Geometry

Grade 8: Geometry

High School:

Modeling

Geometry: Congruence

Similarity, Right Triangles, & Trigonometry

Modeling with Geometry

Procedure: Students have prior knowledge of reflections, but most do not realize the different types of reflection and their mathematical meanings. This activity is geared toward opening their minds to reflections across different axes, as well as making them aware of ways that their prior knowledge of reflections translates into mathematics. Hand out the Anticipation Guide, and instruct students to complete the prereading questions. Use student answers as an opportunity to discuss their prior knowledge, allowing students to respond to each others' answers

Pass out the book *A Mirror to Nature*, and instruct students to begin reading it and looking at the pictures. The book plays on prior knowledge of reflections in water and can be used to demonstrate the various lines of reflection and symmetry. Accompanying the photographs showing reflection are short poems about the photograph's subject.

As students complete the reading, you may instruct them to move to the postreading questions and possibly to re-answer some of their prereading questions. If students want to change their answers, they may do so, leaving the original answers for comparison. The contrast between answers will serve as a learning tool when they realize how their knowledge has developed and changed after reading the story, and again after the content is discussed in class. This short time spent manifesting their prior knowledge will leave students ripe for extending their understanding of transformations in further lessons.

A Mirror to Nature Prereading Questions

1. What is a reflection?

2. What do you think a line of reflection is?

3. Do you think there can be different kinds of lines of reflection?

A Mirror to Nature Postreading Questions

1. What are some similarities between reflections that we see in everyday life and the reflections of shapes that we study in mathematics texts?

2. What is a line of reflection?

3. What are some lines of reflection you observed while reading this book or passage?

LESSON PLAN 2-2

THE UNIVERSAL BOOK OF MATHEMATICS VOCABULARY SQUARE

This is a vocabulary-building exercise that gives multiple representations of the concept behind each vocabulary word in a form that can easily be used and reused as a flashcard.

Materials: Standard size note cards, *The Universal Book of Mathematics* by David Darling or any math dictionary

Duration: 5-10 minutes per vocabulary card

Applicable Common Core Standards

Can be used for vocabulary associated with any of the Common Core standards

Procedure: Pass out note cards so that students have one for each word to be studied. Instruct the students to fold the note card into fourths and label each section, as illustrated in the following example. On the reverse side of the note card, the student should write the vocabulary word only. This allows the note cards to be used as flashcards later. Have multiple dictionaries, such as *The Universal Book of Mathematics*, or student math books available so students can look up the definitions of words they will be studying.

Students should create vocabulary squares as they learn new words in class. Set aside 10 minutes at the end of a lesson for students to create the cards for any new vocabulary. Definitions should be taken from your lesson, the textbook, or a math dictionary. Including the formal definition is important, both for standardized test preparation and for teaching students to formulate their own examples from technical writing sources. The "My Own Words"

(Continued)

LESSON PLAN 2-2 (Continued)

section requires students to create their own version of the word's definition. This part is crucial to helping students understand what the word means in a way that makes sense to them.

When teaching the example, you may choose to use a word found in your students' notes or from their textbook, or even from standardized test practice questions. The picture/memory cue gives students either a visual clue or verbal reminder. Pictures are particularly valuable for students who are more visually oriented, but if the vocabulary word is not well suited to illustration, a verbal cue or an anecdote that was used when you taught the word would suffice.

By the end of a unit, students will have several vocabulary flashcards with many representations, giving both a wide understanding of that unit's vocabulary and a convenient means for reviewing it.

Vocabulary Square Example for "Absolute Value"

Definition	My Own Words
The value of a number without regard to its sign; the distance from zero measured along the real number line	How far a number is away from zero Always a positive number
Example Which of the following values of x make the equation $\lvert -x + 10 \rvert = 8$ true? **a.** 18 **b.** −2 **c.** 2 **d.** −18 **Answer: a**	**Picture or Memory Cue** $\lvert -4 - 4 \rvert$ Place Away from Zero

LESSON PLAN 2-3

THE RED BLAZER GIRLS MULTICOLUMN JOURNAL

The purpose of this triple-entry journal activity is to provide a means for organizing important quotes from a reading, their mathematical significance, and their relevance to the story. It may be adapted to fit any book or topic.

Materials: *The Red Blazer Girls: The Ring of Rocamadour* by Michael Beil, triple-entry journal template

Duration: 1-2 weeks depending on reading level and class time given

---

Applicable Common Core Standards:

Grade 8: Geometry

High School:

Algebra: Reasoning with Equations and Inequalities

   Trigonometric Functions

   Modeling

Procedure: Assign blocks of chapters from the *The Red Blazer Girls: The Ring of Rocamadour* for students to read and collect clues. You may have students read in or outside of class. Clues should include mathematical concepts that will help them solve the mystery of the ring. (The bolded information in the "Clues" column is included to help the students comprehend key material. This feature of the triple-entry journal gives teachers the opportunity to develop their own hints or suggestions to guide student inquiry.)

Set goals throughout reading, having students piece together the mathematics collected in the "Clues" column and demonstrate their skills in the "Solve It" and "Explain" columns. (See example below.) The "Solve It" column gives students an allotted location to substitute variables, combine pieces of information, and solve mathematical problems posed throughout the reading. In addition, the "Explain It" column requires students to make meaning of the mathematics they are doing by narrating their procedures and describing how they decided which procedures were appropriate to use. It is important to mention that students do not have to read the entire novel. Equally productive goals can be achieved by reading excerpts.

By the end of the activity, students will have demonstrated their understanding of a wide variety of mathematical concepts. You may supplement or expand on concepts discussed in the book with short lessons and explanations intended to bolster students' reading comprehension.

Page	Clues	Solve It	Explain
60	(i) + (ii) = (iii) (iv) − (v) = (vi)		
86	**(i)** $= x$ **(ii)** $= 3y$ **(iii)** $= 612 \div d$; where $d =$ distance (rounded to the nearest whole foot)	(i) + (ii) = (iii) $x + 3y = 612 \div d$	I substituted the value of each variable into the equation.

(*Continued*)

LESSON PLAN 2-3 (Continued)

Page	Clues	Solve It	Explain
132	$A = 91$ $B = 46$ **Use the clues collected in Chapters 1 to 19 to complete the first equation.**	 $A^2 + B^2 = C^2$ $(91)^2 + (46)^2 = C^2$ $8{,}281 + 2{,}116 = C^2$ $10{,}397 \div C^2$ $C = 101.97$ $d = 102$ $x + 3y = 612 \div 102$ $x + 3y = 6$	The values that Sophie measured were for each leg of the right triangle. I substituted the values in for A and B in the Pythagorean theorem. Then I added the values, which left me with $B^2 = 10{,}397$ Then I took the square root of both sides on the calculator, which gave me 101.97. The clue says to round to the nearest whole foot, which is 102. The only like terms to combine are $612 \div 102$. I got $d = 102$ from the work done in the previous entry.

    Modifications for Middle School: The heavy use of systems of equations in this text lends it to high school use; however, the middle grades can capitalize on the Pythagorean Theorem and linear equations in the text; simply omit the steps involved in solving the system. The story provides commentary and solutions, so students with less math background will not suffer from lack of comprehension.

References

Alvermann, D. E., & Moore, D. W. (1991). Secondary school reading. In R. Barr, M. L. Kamil, P. B. Mosenthal, & P. D. Pearson (Eds.), *The handbook of reading research* (Vol. 2, pp. 951–983). New York: Longman.

Alvermann, D. E., Phelps, S. F., & Gillis, V. R. (2010). *Content area reading and literacy: Succeeding in today's diverse classrooms.* Boston: Allyn & Bacon.

Carroll, L. (1916). *Alice's adventures in wonderland* (pp. 28–30). New York: Samuel Gabriel Sons and Company. (Original work published in 1865)

Common Core State Standards Initiative. (2010). *Common Core State Standards for English language arts & literacy in history/social studies, science, and technical subjects*. Washington, DC: National Governors Association Center for Best Practices and the Council of Chief State School Officers.

Goodman, K. (1996). *On reading*. Portsmouth, NH: Heinemann.

Hancewicz, E., Heuer, L., Metsisto, D., & Tuttle, C. L. (2005). *Literacy strategies for improving mathematics instruction*. Alexandria, VA: Association for Supervision and Curriculum Development.

Harvey, S., & Goudvis, A. (2000). *Strategies that work: Teaching comprehension to enhance understanding*. Portland, ME: Stenhouse Publishers.

Herber, H. (1978). *Teaching reading in the content areas*. (2nd ed.). Englewood Cliffs, NJ: Prentice-Hall.

Hiebert, J., Gallimore, R., Garnier, H., Givvin, K. B., Hollingsowth, H., Jacobs, J., et al. (2003). *Teaching mathematics in seven countries: Results from the TIMSS 1999 video study, NCES (2003-013)*. Washington, DC: National Center for Educational Statistics.

Koebler, M., & Grouws, D. A. (1992). Mathematics teaching practice and their effects. In D. A. Grouws (Ed.), *Handbook on research of mathematics teaching and learning* (pp. 115–126). New York: Simon & Schuster Macmillan.

Rhodes, L. K., & Shanklin, N. L. (1993). *Windows into literacy: Assessing learners K-8*. Portsmouth, NH: Heinemann.

Smith, F. (2002). *The glass wall: Why mathematics can seem difficult*. New York: Teachers College Press.

Wallace, F. H., Clark, K. K., & Cherry, M. L. (2006). How come? What if? So what? Reading in the mathematics classroom. *Mathematics Teaching in the Middle School, 12*(2), 108–115.

Section II

Exploring Mathematical Text

In this section, we present three chapters that focus on fiction, nonfiction, and picture books. We discuss key features of using fiction, nonfiction, and picture books in the mathematics classroom and provide extensive annotated bibliographies of texts. The inclusion of picture books, in addition to the more general categories of fiction and nonfiction, was an intentional choice to highlight a resource that we believe is underused in the middle and high school grades. While picture books can encompass both fiction and nonfiction, we have chosen to highlight them separately, because their format is unique, blending the text with the illustrations to extend meaning making. Because picture books are a format that is not necessarily tied to any reading level, they can be used in any classroom. The typically brief text of a picture book lends itself particularly well to classroom use.

Each chapter in Section II includes activities that are provided as examples to demonstrate ways teachers might use other books of their choice in the classroom. Suggested strategies for incorporating technology into these literacy activities are also provided. Each chapter discusses key features of using its particular focus—fiction, nonfiction, or picture books—in the mathematics classroom, and each chapter provides extensive annotated bibliographies of texts, including references to Common Core standards.

Chapter 3

Fiction and Mathematical Literacy: Finding Universal Truths in Made-Up Stories

MATHEMATICS IS EVERYWHERE, EVEN IN FAIRY TALES

Most writers of fiction do not set out specifically to educate. Their intent is to entertain. Perhaps, if they are skilled or if they are lucky, they are able to enlighten their audiences along the way. When a story becomes more than just a story, something magical has happened. When a story's characters live their lives in a reader's head, giving the reader the chance to go new places or think new thoughts, then the storyteller has succeeded as an artist. And if those new thoughts involve mathematics, so much the better, as far as the readers of this book are concerned.

But how often is mathematics an obvious part of a fictional plot? Are you accustomed to seeing radicals, numerals, and integrals dotting the pages of novels? No? Then what is the point of this chapter? If novels aren't as obviously math related at first glance as a math textbook is, then how can they be useful in a mathematics classroom?

The answer is simple if you hang tight to a simple fact. Mathematics is everywhere. It describes the shape, motion, and existence of everything. Because this is true, mathematics is implicit in every story ever told.

When Superman fell to Earth, the Kryptonian infant's powerless spaceship traced a parabolic flight trajectory. When Hercules fought the Hydra and two heads appeared in the place of every one that he sliced off, he was fighting the power of a geometric progression. When Rumpelstiltskin made a bet with a desperate queen, he had calculated the probability that she would guess his very unusual name within a 3-day period and deduced that he could not lose.

For the writer of fiction, ignoring mathematical realities results in a story that doesn't *feel* right. Readers notice when a fictional world doesn't operate according to the physical laws that they see every day, even when they don't understand the reason a story makes them feel uncomfortable. For the mathematics teacher, the trick is to learn to see the math that makes the story feel real—and then to show students how to find that math for themselves.

In a book we recommend to all early adolescents, not just math students, *Peter and the Starcatchers* (Barry and Pearson, 2004), you will not find the obvious mathematical references that you will find in some of the other novels. Yet the teacher who knows that this book featuring the exploits of pirates on the high seas is being passed from student to student because it is fun to read can make effective use of that knowledge.

The physics of sailing ships would make a fabulous topic of study. Simple calculations abound, ranging from estimating the pressure of a gale force wind on a large sail to the weight of the water displaced by a pirate ship. More advanced problems involving vectors could also be developed. For example, if a pirate captain wants to travel north, but a three-knot wind is coming from the southwest, what is the maximum speed he can hope to achieve?

Peter's flight trajectory as he flits over the heads of fearsome pirates could be fodder for parabola problems. An assignment to draw a map of his imaginary world, including his ship's path from real-world England to the imaginary Rundoon, would draw on concepts of scale and ratio. These ideas can be applied to any tale of seafaring adventure, from *Treasure Island* (Stevenson,

1883) to the latest bestseller, once a teacher develops a mindset that teases math out of exciting stories. Developing that mindset is the purpose of this book.

Secrets, Lies, and Algebra (see Annotated Bibliographies), on the other hand, does not require a special mindset to see mathematics in the storyline. This book involves math in a completely straightforward manner. A math teacher just has to love a character whose shorthand for her very enthusiastic friend Sammy is s^5, because Sammy takes everything to the fifth power. Books like this, with unambiguous references to math, are valuable resources, but the ability to recognize subtler mathematics references is a key skill for math teachers hoping to incorporate fiction in their classrooms.

The Parrot's Theorem (see Annotated Bibliographies) was selected because it presents yet another way fiction can enhance the study of mathematics. It presents a concise but comprehensive history of mathematics, tucked into a story about a family enduring hard times. The history of mathematics is sometimes neglected in favor of the "doing" of mathematics, but students whose interests lean toward the social sciences can often become more engaged in math studies when they're made to understand the importance of mathematics in our culture.

Peruse the list of recommended books in the Annotated Bibliographies for ideas, and then consider the sample activity that concludes this chapter. It was taken from a novel marketed to adult readers of mysteries, and yet there is unmistakably math-related content at the very heart of this story—a beloved character is nearly killed by the clever use of ratios.

Try these books in your classroom. There's a probability that your students will learn math to a degree that's disproportionate to the number of factorials in the narrative. But first, the following two boxes discuss some observations on fiction in the mathematics classroom, the first one written by a working classroom teacher and the second written by an author whose books have been successfully used as resources by math teachers.

Activity: Comments from the Classroom

by Alyson Lischka

In the popular novel *The Hunger Games* by Suzanne Collins, the author sprinkles mathematical detours appropriate for middle and high school mathematics students into the first chapter. While the story itself is not directly mathematical, the topics of problem solving, unit measurement, and probability are present in the opening. The novel centers on the probability of selection of two Tributes from a region of the fictional country Panem to participate in the brutal Hunger Games where Tributes fight to the death.

The introduction of the novel's lead character, Katniss Everdeen, takes place as she hunts and gathers food with her longtime friend Gale. They fish and gather berries and greens to feed their families. Returning to market with their goods, Katniss and Gale keep some of the day's harvest and trade the rest for items such as salt, bread, and money. For the early mathematics learner, it would be good practice to have students follow the various measures of the items and verify that they agree with each other

(Continued)

throughout the chapter. This will entail some unit conversion. Further, problem-solving skills such as careful reading and verification of solutions can be practiced as students trace the passage of goods throughout the chapter.

Collins also weaves the topic of probability throughout the opening chapter of the novel. Shortly after Gale is introduced, he proclaims, "Happy Hunger Games! . . . And may the odds – be ever in your favor!" (p. 8). Later on in the chapter, we learn of the practice called "the reaping" where Tributes' names are drawn to participate in the games. There is a complex system determining which names are in the pool of choices and how many times each name is entered. This process, deemed unfair by Katniss, is replete with topics in probability that could be tied to probability standards presented at all levels of the Common Core standards.

Even without discussing any mathematical calculations, the terminology used by Gale and Katniss (*odds* and *unfair*) leads to interesting conversations. How do odds relate to probability? Are they the same idea or different? What makes a game unfair? Does unfair have a mathematical meaning, or is it simply a subjective idea? All of these questions are important ideas for students to understand and conceptualize when learning about probability. It is important to note that, although these two terms are used frequently in common language, there are mathematical ideas tied directly to them that do not always match their use in common language.

With a little elaboration, one could further explore the idea of probability within the depicted reaping process. Although the total number in the population is not given in the novel, a total could be chosen. Then an estimate for the number of children in that population between the ages of 12 and 18 (the ages for participation in the reaping) can be made. One could set up a hypothetical population and have students explore the probability of Gale's name or Katniss' name being drawn from the pool. Classroom simulations are a powerful way for students to begin exploring simple probability, singly or collaboratively. Tying that exploration to a novel makes the simulation even more potent.

Finding Math Where You Least Expect It

by Mary Anna Evans

My late father always said, "No education is ever wasted." I find myself quoting him often when I'm asked to explain why I left my engineering and physics education behind to write novels. This is a valid question, if the questioner presumes that differential equations and parabolic flight trajectories have nothing to do with my stories. But I write crime fiction, and parabolic flight trajectories describe the paths of bullets and the motion of a falling body. Differential equations govern the combustion of the compounds in the kerosene used by an arsonist to burn down a house.

Do I force my readers to slog through those differential equations or trace those flight paths? Of course not. I write to entertain, not to bore. But becoming a novelist did not require me to wipe my memory clean of the things I learned in engineering school, and I believe I write different stories than I would have written if I'd skipped the science education and gone straight into writing. What you know affects who you are, and who you are affects what you write. You can never escape the things you've put into your brain.

And so, shortly after my first book, *Artifacts*, came out, I had the surreal experience of receiving an email from my high school geometry teacher, Beth Harrison. (Clearly, Beth was very, very young when she taught me.) She said, "There's geometry in this book!!!" And I said, "No, there's not!!!" So she said, "Check page 200." And there it was: an x-y plane in the form of surveying flags laid out in a regular grid.

Shortly after that, I googled *Artifacts*, and I found that it was being used in a high school in Connecticut, far from my home in Florida. I was curious, so I clicked around on the school's website and discovered that *Artifacts* had been selected by Voice of Youth Advocates (VOYA) for its annual list of "Adult Mysteries with Young Adult Appeal." (Perhaps it will tell you something about a writer's importance in the general scheme of things when you realize that no one had thought to tell me this wonderful news.)

After this, the serendipitous series of events that have brought me to this book began. Through Beth, I met educational consultants who showed me wonderful ways that popular fiction like my books could be used to teach mathematics (and all subjects, really). I traveled with them to educators' conferences, talking about how to marry math and literature in a way that will engage student interest. My second book, *Relics*, received a lovely review from *School Library Journal*. I received an invitation from the high school on the Choctaw reservation near Philadelphia, Mississippi, to speak to their faculty about ways to incorporate the Choctaw history and culture in my third book, *Effigies*, into their classrooms, and this school visit might well be the most emotionally satisfying response to my work that I've yet received.

In the midst of this excitement, I met my friend and colleague, Dr. Faith Wallace, and we embarked on a series of proposals, presentations, and articles that eventually became this book. Could I have possibly planned this adventure when I sat down to begin writing *Artifacts* a decade ago? Of course not. Would I change a thing? Oh, heavens, no.

What have I learned from this experience? I've learned that, although the thought of math never crossed my mind when I was writing my books, I put geometry in *Artifacts*, those pesky parabolic flight trajectories in *Relics*, deadly ratios in *Effigies*, Cartesian coordinates in *Findings*, fluid mechanics in *Floodgates*, and the simple arithmetic of time in *Strangers*.

I post lesson plans for my books on my website, www.maryannaevans.com, because I adore knowing that young people are learning the math so dear to my heart by reading the books into which I have poured my heart. (When I check the analytics for my site, I see that search strings like "character list for artifacts" or "important themes in effigies" have brought people to the site, and I know that students are looking for shortcuts to completing their homework, as they have for all of recorded time. Rest assured that I have not made it *quite* that easy to pull the wool over their teachers' eyes.)

What else have I learned from this experience? I've been forcibly reminded how intimately math is bound into our daily lives. Mathematics describes . . . well . . . everything. If students can learn to see geometry embedded in their favorite video games and if they can recognize the algebra implicit in the motion of their first car, then the equations in their textbooks will make more sense.

Most of all, I have been reminded how beautiful math is, as purely beautiful as the curves of a flowering vine twined around the trunk of a longleaf pine tree. If a mathematics education can keep my eyes open to the wonder in this world where we walk for such a short time, then that education was not wasted. Thanks for explaining that to me, Daddy.

ANNOTATED BIBLIOGRAPHIES

Fiction Recommended for Middle Grade Math Classes

The Unknowns by Benedict Carey
Amulet Books, 2009

Something is wrong in the town of Adjacent; slowly, people are just disappearing, but no one seems to notice. That is, until Lady Di Smith and Tom Jones learn that their friend and tutor, Mrs. Clarke, is the next person to go missing. Lady Di and Tom know Mrs. Clarke wouldn't just leave and believe that the plant where everyone works is behind the disappearances. When they go to investigate, they find she left them a clue in the form of a number riddle, but how can three plus four equal five? And the adventure begins.

Lady Di and Tom, using different thinking processes, realize that they are dealing with a triangle and are rewarded when they begin middle school and learn about the Pythagorean theorem. Clue after clue poses mathematical problems, from plotting points on a coordinate plane to solving an equation for slope, but the clues aren't just about solving a mathematical problem. As Lady Di and Tom enlist the help of their friends, the author is careful to show how the group works collaboratively to come up with solutions that make sense given what they know. They test their hypothesis and rework problems. Mathematical concepts and vocabulary are peppered throughout this adventure starting with the name of the town, Adjacent, and even the names of characters, Rene D. Quartez and Pascal Blasè. Diagrams, charts, and graphs are included throughout the text to further illustrate the mathematics.

While the mathematics is rich, the story is engaging. The characters, all outsiders, become friends as they solve clues and protect each other from a gang of bullies called The Poets. Each clue takes them through underground (and under garbage) tunnels posing terrible danger, but if they stick together, they just might become heroes.

The Red Blazer Girls: The Ring of Rocamadour by Michael D. Beil
Random House, 2009

During English class, Sophie, staring out the window at the adjacent church, sees something strange enough to make her scream in the middle of class. When she, Margaret, and Rebecca decide to investigate, they find a secret passage from the church leading to the Harriman residence, where Mrs. Harriman is waiting for them. She needs their help to solve a family mystery involving an ancient treasure. The first clue has been found and will set the girls on a scavenger hunt throughout the school and church using their knowledge of literature, math, religion, and more.

Sophie and her friends are excited to become super-sleuths, but suddenly, the clues become confusing. The second clue is an equation, but the equation isn't straightforward—it has its own clues to solve. The girls work through riddles, formulas, and equations, and they are rewarded with a treasure map of sorts. The treasure is the ancient and priceless Ring of Rocamadour that

Mrs. Harriman's father left for his granddaughter when she was Sophie's age. The legend of the ring is that it can grant wishes, and the girls are determined to find it.

Can the girls unravel the mystery of the map to find the treasure? With one last mystery to solve, the girls must brush up on their knowledge of coordinate plane geometry, solve their equations, plot their points, and find the precise intersection of the resulting lines on the floor of the church.

Time is running out, someone else is hot on their tails, looking for that ring, and demolition on the church is about to start. Who can the girls trust to help them before it is too late? Can they find the treasure and reunite the Harriman family at the same time? This book is a fun interdisciplinary mystery with lots of charm.

Secrets, Lies, and Algebra by Wendy Lichtman
HarperCollins, 2007

Tess, the protagonist of this young adult mystery, is a very bright girl who looks at the world in terms of mathematics. This eighth grader's world revolves around very common adolescent concerns—Are her friends trustworthy? Where does she stand in her school's pecking order? How should she behave when she sees that her parents aren't infallible?—but she interprets those concerns in terms of Venn diagrams and polynomials.

Any adolescent will recognize Tess's interpretation of the equation for school popularity (where T = Tess and R = Richard, then T < R, T > R, or T = R), and any adolescent will resonate with Tess's commentary on these relationships: "In math, if a number is greater or less than another one, that never changes. The inequality $11 > 7$ is always true, for example. But with people, that's not the way it works." This entertaining book is a quick read with much fodder for discussion in the mathematics classroom.

Secrets, Lies, and Algebra is the first in a series of math-related young adult novels planned by Wendy Lichtman. The second in the series, *The Writing on the Wall*, was published by HarperCollins in 2008.

Fiction Recommended for High School Math Classes

The Hunger Games by Suzanne Collins
Scholastic Press, 2008

The Hunger Games is a dystopian thriller set in Appalachia, after the fall of our civilization and the rise of another, centered around a capital in the Rockies. Thirteen outlying districts rebelled against this new government and were crushed. One district was destroyed outright, as an example to the survivors, and the remaining twelve districts are kept under tight governmental control. Hunger—real hunger—is rampant, and starvation is an undeniable possibility for anyone who falls on hard times.

As an ever-present reminder of their subjugation, the conquered people must endure an annual reaping. Two teenaged representatives from each district are taken to the capital city to compete to the death in the Hunger Games.

Only one of the twenty-four contestants will live. The tag line for these games, "May the odds be ever in your favor," encapsulates the mathematical thrust of this book. What are any child's chances of being reaped? And what are the odds that any contestant will survive? Gambling on the victor is yet another way that the ruling classes exploit these children.

The mathematical content is less robust than in other books recommended here, but the story is so compelling that we have found it worthwhile to suggest ways to incorporate it into the math classroom. The first two chapters, during which the reader learns about the reaping and sees one in action, could be read in class, as background for a discussion of the ways the rules of the reaping affect a given child's odds of winning—or losing. It's not just a matter of pulling a name out of a hat, with each person bearing an equal chance of hearing his or her name called. Older children's names are entered more times, and families who are in danger of starving can get extra food if they're willing to enter a child's name another time . . . and another . . . and another.

Teachers who opt to have their students read the entire book can amplify this discussion by talking about the factors that improve a contestant's chance of survival—the score on a precompetition exhibition of survival skills, the ability to appeal to the audience for assistance by being attractive or fierce, and the ability to outsmart the Gamemakers. Working in conjunction with the students' English teacher to read the book for both classes is also an option. Our guess is that, even if students are only required to read and discuss the probability lesson implicit in the first two chapters, they will go on to finish this gripping book on their own.

Catching Fire and *Mockingjay* complete *The Hunger Games* trilogy.

The Parrot's Theorem by Denis Guedj, Translated by Frank Wynne
Thomas Dunne Books, 2000

The Parrot's Theorem is a uniquely charming book. The math presented is sophisticated, and it is embedded in a history of mathematics that is quite comprehensive, given the limited space in which it is presented. This is especially true when considering the space allotted to the story of a nontraditional family living in an apartment above a Parisian bookstore.

This book is intentionally presented immediately after *The Hunger Games*, as they represent a sharp contrast in style and mathematics content. Whereas *The Hunger Games* is a page turner, with some mathematical content that is not the primary focus of the book, *The Parrot's Theorem*, is a slow-moving tale that takes a leisurely approach to the tale of Perrette and her three children and the elderly bookseller who is slowly becoming part of their family—and their parrot, who just might know the solution to two of mathematics' most famous unsolved mysteries.

This book is recommended without reservation to mathematics teachers for their own reading, as there are many stories from the history of mathematics that are worthy of inclusion in the classroom. Classroom reading of excerpts from the text would provide opportunities to put the most important discoveries in mathematics into an easily readable classroom context. A reading of the entire text might be more appropriate for advanced students, as the writing style is dense, both in terms of language and in terms of math. But for students with an appreciation for the wonder of mathematics, time spent with this parrot will be well rewarded.

Denis Guedj is the author of several other French-language books related to mathematics. Two of them, both aimed at the adult market, have been translated into English—*Numbers: The Universal Language* and *The Measure of the World: A Novel*.

The Square Root of Murder by Camille Minichino
Berkley, 2011

Camille Minichino holds a doctorate in physics, and she has an abiding interest in mathematical literacy for nonmathematicians. It shows in her work. *The Square Root of Murder* is the first installment in her new series of mysteries featuring puzzle enthusiast and mathematics professor Dr. Sophie Knowles. The fictional Sophie teaches workshops for college students with mathematics anxiety, and she constructs puzzles at all levels of difficulty, which she publishes under a pseudonym to avoid the disapproval of her strait-laced department chair. Reading a book written from Sophie's point of view will put students into the head of a person who is completely comfortable in the world of numbers, yet who feels a need to reach out to people who are intimidated by math.

In Sophie's words, "The truth was that, given the right teacher, anyone could learn mathematics. One of my greatest missions in life was to help students over hurdles that kept them thinking that there was a certain 'science brain' or that only a select few had a 'knack for math.'" When one of Sophie's university colleagues is murdered in his office, Sophie's knack for logic, as well as her concern for a friend who is under suspicion, drives her to seek a solution to the mystery that fits the facts.

The Square Root of Murder is aimed at the adult market, but it is appropriate for recommending to secondary students looking for pleasure reading that features an appealing mathematician and is sprinkled with references to great mathematicians in history. Additional mathematics-related mysteries featuring Dr. Sophie Knowles are planned.

Dr. Minichino's earlier series, *The Periodic Table Mysteries*, offers a similar tour through the world of chemistry.

Conned Again, Watson!: Cautionary Tales of Logic, Math, and Probability by Colin Bruce
Vintage, 2001

Colin Bruce, a physicist and an expert in mathematical paradoxes, allows the familiar team of Sherlock Holmes and Dr. Watson to tell these tales of probability and surprise. In each story, a client asks the investigatory team to investigate a situation in which common sense suggests one result, yet reality has given—or is about to give—another.

A common theme explored time and again in this collection is the notion that our instincts for the probability of any given outcome are usually quite poor. When faced with a coin that has been flipped twenty times, coming up heads every time, most people feel quite safe in betting that the coin will come up tails on the next flip, because they believe the odds of this result are very high. And most people would be wrong. The odds of tossing tails are 50% every time a coin is flipped because a coin has no memory of the results of previous tosses. Many fortunes have been lost to the erroneous understanding of probability questions like this one.

In these twelve stories, Bruce lays out twelve scenarios, and then walks the reader through the surprising logic that underpins them. The short story format lends itself to the classroom, providing self-contained readings that can be accomplished in a single class period. Young readers who pay close attention will be exposed to twelve classic probability problems, and they'll also be far less likely in the future to lose a fortune—or even a dime—to a huckster who presumes that they lack mathematical understanding.

Bruce is also the author of *The Strange Case of Mrs. Hudson's Cat, or Sherlock Holmes Solves the Einstein Mysteries* and *The Einstein Paradox: And Other Science Mysteries Solved by Sherlock Holmes*, in which the detective and his physician sidekick delve into issues of modern physics, relativity, and quantum physics.

Anathem by Neal Stephenson
Morrow, 2008

Anathem is a world-building—no, a cosmos-building—saga that unfolds over 900 pages of densely written text, and here is the lone problem with recommending this text for the classroom. The time required to read it is a large investment, but a worthwhile one for advanced secondary students of mathematics, because the cosmos being built by author Stephenson is based heavily on math, particularly geometry. It is a tale of a future universe—or is it a parallel future universe?—where mathematical knowledge is preserved over successive dark ages in monastery-like cloisters known as "maths." The faith of these brothers and sisters, called "fraas" and "suurs," lies in the purity of concepts like the isosceles triangle, and they have voluntarily locked themselves away from a society very much like ours in order to focus on developing their understanding of these timeless truths.

When an unprecedented crisis from beyond the walls of his math forces the very appealing protagonist, Fraa Erasmus, to enter the everyday world, the value of his theoretical education becomes clear. Few teachers will resist applauding when Erasmus is told that, although he has been shut away from technology for 10 of his 18 years, he is the ideal candidate for a high-tech jaunt into space because he has spent those 18 years making himself educable.

This book is recommended as a supplemental text to be assigned to motivated students for outside reading. In-class activities could include a reading and discussion of excerpts; a good example would be pages 15 through 25, a description of the architecture of Fraa Erasmus' math. Students could then be invited to discuss or sketch or model their understanding of this complex building, from the pillars that are " . . . not round in cross-section, but stretched out diagonally, almost as if they were fins on an old-fashioned rocketship . . . " (p. 19), to the cubic, octahedral, dodecahedral, and icosahedral weights that run the community's clock (p. 21).

Other books by Stephenson include *Cryptonomicon*, featuring a mathematician/cryptographer, and a series known as *The Baroque Cycle*, featuring the conflict between Newton and Leibniz over credit for the development of calculus. All of Stephenson's books share the difficulty of being very long and densely written for easy incorporation into the classroom, but they offer rewards for motivated students or for educators interested in delving into the rich stories for excerpts of appropriate length for the classroom.

Fantasia Mathematica by Clifton Fadiman
Simon & Schuster, 1958

Fantasia Mathematica is a compilation of short stories, poems, and essays with a common theme—they are based on mathematical themes, but they stand as worthy examples of their individual art forms. For this reason, this book might have been included in the poetry or nonfiction chapters, but, well, we had to put it somewhere, and it seems best suited to fiction, as the bulk of the volume is devoted to short stories.

The relatively early publication date of 1958 results in a somewhat dated feel to some of the selections. This fact, along with the sophistication of the language used in those selections, prompts us to point out that this book is probably better suited for older and/or more advanced students. For those appropriate classes, however, this book gives a wide selection of works of a length that is eminently manageable for classroom use.

Due to the age of the book, many of the short stories are from the time period known as the Golden Age of Science Fiction. Teaming with an English class that is studying this period would be an excellent way to explore the overlap between mathematics and literature.

Clifton Fadiman compiled a similar volume in 1962, *The Mathematical Magpie*.

Effigies by Mary Anna Evans, The Faye Longchamp Archaeological Mystery Series
Poisoned Pen Press, 2007

Effigies is the third installment of Mary Anna Evans' series of mysteries featuring archaeologist Faye Longchamp. Although marketed for adults, the series has found an audience in the young adult world, beginning when the first book, *Artifacts*, was chosen by VOYA for its annual list of "Adult Mysteries with Young Adult Appeal." (See the box by Mary Anna Evans, earlier in this chapter, for more background on how she learned about this unexpected audience for her work.)

While mathematical content can be gleaned from all the books in this series, *Effigies* is highlighted here because the murderer chooses a method of dispatching the victim that is a very straightforward demonstration of the power of ratios in understanding the world. It is also well suited for teaching across the curriculum, having won praise from *Booklist* for its incorporation of history, saying, "Evans adds an extra layer of substance to her series by drawing readers into the fascinating history of ancient American civilizations," and from *Publishers Weekly* for literary techniques suitable for discussion in English classes: " . . . her sympathetic characters and fascinating archeological lore add up to a style all her own." Lesson plans available on her website, www.maryannaevans.com, include integrated lessons allowing math, English, and social sciences classes to read *Effigies* and then explore subjects as diverse as ratios, Native American folk tales, and the Trail of Tears.

Other books in the series are *Artifacts, Relics, Findings, Floodgates, Strangers,* and *Plunder.*

LESSON PLAN 3-1

THE WRONG RATIO CAN BE DEADLY: AN INVESTIGATION OF RATIOS BASED ON *EFFIGIES*

This enrichment activity illustrates the real-world applications of mathematical knowledge, while encouraging students to read and comprehend a story that shows the potentially serious ramifications of a mathematical mistake. Students are familiar with medications and dosage, giving them a concrete understanding of the ways that ratios are important in day-to-day life.

Materials: Worksheet/pencils, *Effigies* (Evans, 2007)
Duration: 45-60 minutes or homework assignment

Applicable Common Core Standards:

Grade 6: Ratios and Proportional Relationships

   Expressions and Equations

Grade 7: Ratios and Proportional Relationships

   The Number System

   Expressions and Equations

High School:

Algebra: Seeing Structure in Expressions

   Creating Equations

   Reasoning with Equations and Inequalities

Functions: Linear, Quadratic, and Exponential Models

   Modeling

Procedure: Students should have learned how to set up and solve proportions before this lesson plan is used, so you will be expanding on the real-world applications in this lesson. Discuss the book's plot as it relates to the ratio problem, and then hand out worksheets and ask students to read the excerpt.

The real-world application of proportions can seem a little overwhelming, so it is recommended that you allow students to work with partners or in small groups. Encourage them to use their notes on proportions while completing the activity. Upon completion of this activity, students will have worked a series of problems illustrating the application of ratios to a very important real-life issue—preventing overdoses by correctly calculating drug dosages.

Excerpt from *Effigies*

A tiny plop sounded somewhere to Faye's left, reminding her that, though the prehistoric engineers' work had survived an astonishingly long time, the ceiling above her was exceedingly frail. If one more rock fell out of that ceiling and dropped noisily into the water, she planned to scream. Except Faye found screaming oddly unsatisfying when none of the sound reflected off the earthen walls of her prison.

On the plus side, she'd found that the deadened silence focused her mind. She'd figured out how Neely managed to tamper with Mr. Judd's pills, even though she wasn't in possession of a pharmacist's license.

It all fit together so nicely now. She could see the sheriff's hands competently sorting the pills. Nobody could have known the medications of an aging man better than Neely. At a guess, Faye would say that Mr. Rutland weighed twice as much as the congressman, and he was a lot sicker. She was no doctor, but surely the dosage of his blood pressure medicine would have to be at least twice as high as Mr. Judd's, maybe a lot more.

By filling her father's prescription and giving it to Judd, Neely had nearly committed the world's easiest, most bloodless murder. Of course, Mr. Judd had suffered a catastrophic drop in blood pressure. He was given a significant overdose of a drug designed to lower blood pressure. If he'd died of the overdose, as Neely had planned, his body would have gone undiscovered till morning. He survived because Faye was knocking on his door at the very moment he collapsed. Five minutes later, he'd have been unconscious and unable to answer her.

She'd rushed him to the hospital, where they'd overlooked the discrepancy in the dosage and sent him home . . . so he could take the same overdose again. And five more over strong doses waited in his pill case. If Sallie Judd and his doctors couldn't figure out what had happened—and why would his doctors suspect such a thing?—he would take an overdose again as soon as he was released from the hospital. And he'd do it every day, until those high-dosage pills were gone, or until he died. If Faye and Joe and Oka Hofobi died, there would be no one to warn him. (Evans, 2007, p. 259)

Ratio Problems Based on Concepts Presented in *Effigies*

1. You were told in the excerpt that Neely's father weighs twice as much as Mr. Judd. If the two men were supposed to take the same dosage of

(*Continued*)

LESSON PLAN 3-1 (Continued)

the blood pressure medication—for example, 20 milligrams per 10 kilo-grams—how large an overdose did Mr. Judd take when he took Neely's father's pills by mistake?

a. Four times his normal dose

b. Two times his normal dose

c. Ten times his normal dose

Answer: b. This question is presented in such a way that the student can work the problem conceptually (and probably instinctively), deducing that since Neely's father is twice Mr. Judd's weight, his dosage must be twice the smaller man's. The student is also given enough information to check this answer mathematically. Assume any number for Mr. Judd's weight—for example, 75 kilograms. This yields a value of 150 kilograms for Neely's father's weight. Using the example ratio, 20 milligrams per 10 kilograms, Mr. Judd's dosage is 150 milligrams and Neely's father's dosage is 300 mil-ligrams, or twice Mr. Judd's normal dose.

2. According to the excerpt, Neely's father is much sicker than Mr. Judd, so it is possible that he needed a larger dose to keep his blood pressure down. If he weighs twice as much as Mr. Judd and his dosage is twice as strong—for example, 40 milligrams per 10 kilograms—how large an overdose did Mr. Judd get by mistakenly taking Neely's father's pills?

Answer: The overdose would be four times as strong as the proper dose. Again, some students will be able to calculate this in their head. To calculate it using arithmetic, choose any weight for the two men. We will continue to use 75 kilograms for Mr. Judd and 150 kilograms for Neely's father. At a rate of 40 milligrams per 10 kilograms, Neely's father's dose would be 600 milligrams, as compared to Mr. Judd's dosage of 150 milligrams, calcu-lated as part of Question 1.

3. If Mr. Judd's dose should be 4 milligrams per 10 kilograms, and he weighs 70 kilograms, how many milligrams of the drug should he take?

Answer: This problem can be solved by setting up equivalent ratios.

$$\frac{4 \text{ mg}}{10 \text{ kg}} = \frac{x \text{ mg}}{70 \text{ kg}}$$

By cross-multiplying, we get $10x = 280$, or **28 milligrams**

4. Suppose Mr. Judd weighs 163 pounds and Neely's father weighs 337 pounds. What is the ratio of Mr. Judd's weight to Neely's father's weight? What is the ratio of Neely's father's weight to Mr. Judd's weight?

Answer: The ratio of Mr. Judd's weight to Neely's father's weight is **163:337**.

The ratio of Neely's father's weight to Mr. Judd's weight is **337:163**.

5. There are 2.2 pounds in a kilogram. If you were to take a medication at a ratio of 15 milligrams per kilogram, how much should you take?

Answer: To solve this problem, the student should convert his or her weight to kilograms, by dividing the number of pounds by 2.2. Multiplying that result by 15 milligrams per kilogram yields a dosage for that student's weight.

References

Beil, M. (2009). *The red blazer girls: the ring of rocamadour*. New York: Random House.

Bruce, C. (2001). *Conned again, Watson!: cautionary tales of logic, math, and probability*. New York: Vintage.

Carey, B. (2009). *The unknowns* by Benedict Carey. New York:Amulet Books.

Collins, S. (2008). *The hunger games*. New York: Scholastic Press.

Common Core State Standards Initiative. (2010). *Common Core State Standards for English language arts & literacy in history/social studies, science, and technical subjects*. Washington, DC: National Governors Association Center for Best Practices and the Council of Chief State School Officers.

Evans, M.A. (2007). *Effigies*. Scottsdale, AZ: Poisoned Pen Press.

Fadiman, C. (1958). *Fantasia mathematica*. New York: Simon & Schuster.

Guedj, D. & Wynne, F. (2000). New York: Thomas Dunne Books.

Lichtmann, W. (2007). *Secrets, lies, and algebra*. New York: HarperCollins.

Minichino, C. (2011). *The square root of murder*. New York: Berkley, 2011

Stephenson, N. (2008). *Anathem*. New York: Morrow.

Stevenson, R.L. (1883.) *Treasure island*. New York: C. Scribner's Sons.

Chapter 4

Nonfiction: The Place Where True Stories and Mathematics Intersect

INTRODUCTION

Generally, we think of nonfiction as being informational text, whether it is found in a reference book, concept book, biography, how-to manual, or activity book. Most adults read nonfiction in the form of magazines, newspapers, and even blogs, but the reading patterns of young adults differ widely.

Take a moment to browse what your students are reading. While many are reading fiction, others will be devouring urban legends, weird-but-true stories, or books about magic, ghosts, or paranormal activity. Still others are reading celebrity biographies or companion books to movies and television shows. There is a certain amount of joy to be had in reading informational texts, especially when those facts are fascinating to the young mind. So why do students balk at reading a textbook?

The answer is somewhat simple. Classroom textbooks are dry, lengthy, and full of exercises, homework, and study guides. Works of nonfiction (sometimes called informational trade books), on the other hand, are written by authors passionate about a topic. They write with the intention of grabbing your attention, providing little-known but compelling details, linking the subject to everyday life experiences, and, often, providing captivating illustrations to support the topic at hand. Trade books are written for the general public and are not necessarily intended for use as a school textbook or aligned with any specific standards. Trade books are to be enjoyed, so there are no test questions or other accompanying assessments to be graded. And why should there be?

Can you remember a time, as an adult, when you read a work of nonfiction for pleasure and were then handed a quiz on what you read? Probably not. But such texts can greatly enhance the study of mathematics at the middle and high school grades when chosen carefully to meet the level of student reading, interest, and content being studied. Because nonfiction trade books encompass a wide range of formats and styles, they are extremely versatile in the classroom. From a short sidebar linking a concept to everyday life to an orderly list of details on how to play a game, teachers will find new and interesting ways to use nonfiction trade books in middle and high school math classrooms.

ANNOTATED BIBLIOGRAPHY OF NONFICTION BOOKS SUITABLE FOR MIDDLE AND HIGH SCHOOL CLASSES

Activity Books

A popular type of nonfiction or informational trade book is an activity book where students can work through a set of instructions to engage in a creative activity. *Mastering Math Through Magic* (Lombardo, 2003) is a perfect example of an activity book. Middle grade students are provided with step-by-step directions to learn how to perform magic such as guessing someone's age, determining the number rolled on a random die, or even picking out someone's favorite number. The teacher introduction explains, "As students focus on learning magic tricks, they don't realize that they are improving their knowledge of how numbers work along with practicing basic math skills" (p. vi).

Similarly, *40 Fabulous Math Mysteries Kids Can't Resist* (Lee & Miller, 2001) invites readers to try to solve engaging short mysteries using mathematics. The introduction explains, "Good problems get kids to think mathematically. They require students to apply number sense and intuitive thinking skills, explore patterns, make and test reasonable estimates, show flexibility in thinking, adjust assumptions, work backwards, use manipulatives, make sketchings, and even act out situations" (p. 5). Mathematical topics for the mysteries in this book include number and operations, measurement, algebra, geometry, data applications, probability, and reasoning. The mysteries are short enough that several can be completed in one class period. While some activity books focus more heavily on practicing problem solving, the problems are always presented in unique ways such as through comic strips, stories, or links to everyday life. What follows is an annotated bibliography of activity books that can supplement mathematics classroom instruction.

200 Super-Fun, Super-Fast Math Story Problems by Dan Greenberg
Scholastic, 2002

With a humorous slant on story problems, this book takes everyday situations (for example, weather, computers, movies, and even pets) and turns them into mathematical problems where students can practice their prowess in multiplication, division, fractions, decimals, measurement, and more. The book is arranged not by topic, but by month, so that teachers can use a problem a day for an interesting way to start or finish class. Use the problems as challenges or just for fun. Each problem is labeled with the mathematical skill being highlighted. While the difficulty level makes these problems more appropriate for middle grade classes, students of all ages will enjoy the puzzle-like problem solving provided.

The Big Book of Brain Games: 1,000 Play Thinks of Art, Mathematics & Science by Ivan Moscovich and Ian Stewart
Workman Publishing Group, 2006

Students won't get bored with these 1,000 cross-curriculum games, including puzzles, riddles, and illusions. The book is divided into twelve different categories, and the math categories include geometry, patterns, numbers, logic and probability, and perception. Each game is ranked for difficulty, making it user-friendly to students of all ages. All of the solutions to the games can be located at the back of the book for easy reference. This collection of games was made possible by a group of mathematicians, scientists, inventors, and even magicians who were all fascinated by the intersection of mind games and mathematics. Mathematical topics include geometry, points and lines, graphs and networks, curves and circles, shapes and polygons, and more.

Comic-Strip Math by Dan Greenberg
Scholastic, 1998

Comic-Strip Math includes the types of comic strips found in the newspaper, without the reliance on superheroes and action. The comic strips are short enough to keep students interested, while encouraging them to pay attention to the language in the comic strip in order to solve the presented mathematical problem. The introduction explains, "Using funny characters and a whimsical point of view, the cartoons on these pages explore a variety of critical mathematical topics . . . . Topics focus on basic number operation . . . and cover such elements as fractions, decimals, estimation, mental math, measurement, geometry, and graphing" (p. 8).

Fantasy Baseball and Mathematics: A Resource Guide for Teachers and Parents by Dan Flockhart
Jossey-Bass, 2007

This book is part of a series on Fantasy Sports and Mathematics including basketball, football, and soccer. The purpose of this activity book is to encourage students to use mathematics to calculate both player and team statistics. Students begin by creating their own fantasy baseball team, choosing from major league players. Over the course of the season, students track the progress of their fantasy team using mathematical skills such as algebra, statistics, and more. Over 100 scoring systems are available for students to keep track of the progress of their team. The introduction to the book explains, *"Fantasy Baseball and Mathematics* is a game in which participants create and manage teams of professional baseball players. Players earn points for hits, walks, stolen bases, home runs, runs scored, and runs batted in. Players lose points for striking out or making errors. Each week, students find the sum of the points earned by their players, using one of the scorings suggested in the book" (p. 3). There is a unique technological tie-in because many smart phones, such as the iPhone, have applications that are specifically designed to keep track of baseball scores.

Hands-On Math Projects with Real-Life Applications by Judith A. Muschla and Gary Robert Muschla
Jossey-Bass, 2006

This activity book is designed completely around mathematical activities that are rooted in real-life situations. With careful detail on how to use these activities in the classroom, this book not only delivers on the activities, but also on classroom management, encouraging team projects and self-assessments. The collection of projects ranges from exploring games that young adults play all over the world to designing a quilt pattern to planning and sticking to a budget. Cross-curriculum activities are also included, integrating math and science, social studies, and language arts.

The Math Book for Girls and Other Beings Who Count by Valerie Wyatt
Kids Can Press, 2000

This book features NORA (Natural Observation Research Activator) as the fairy godmother. She is responsible for creating situations throughout the book that use math in real-world applications. The short scenarios keep readers' attention and provide motivation for completing the mathematics activities involving subjects such as areas of irregular shapes, nets of three-dimensional objects, and probability. This is an excellent way to encourage girls in your class to think about the math in their daily lives.

Math Games & Activities from Around the World by Claudia Zaslavsky
Chicago Review Press, 1998

This book is full of descriptions and directions for playing over seventy games from around the world that all involve math. Learn to play games from Kenya, Ghana, New Zealand, Mexico, and more. One entire chapter focuses on the geometry all around us from the Olympic symbol to the Chinese yin-yang symbol to the Parthenon in Greece.

   Mathematics comes into play in a variety of ways. The introduction explains, "In all of these activities you will be using math. Many of these math ideas are probably different from the math you learn in school. If a puzzle or activity doesn't work out at first, just keep trying. Read the hints and suggestions carefully" (p. viii). Games of chance and strategy are included, some requiring multiple players, game boards, dice, or other pieces. A second book, *More Math Games & Activities from Around the World*, was published in 2003.

Mind Games: Number Games by Ivan Moscovich
Workman Publishing Company, 2000

With puzzles, games, and toys, this book is for those students who are ready for the challenge of solving mathematical problems covering geometry, symmetry, fractal points, and lines. Some of the games involve magic squares, hexagons, and triangles. This book contains 25 mind-challenging games and puzzles that will force students to rethink what they believe they know about mathematics. Author Ivan Moscovich explains that the activities challenge readers to think about the ways to develop strategies and to search for interesting patterns.

Real Life Math Mysteries by Marya Washington Tyler
Prufrock Press, 1995

Any professional, from a politician to a pilot to an archaeologist, needs an on-the-job understanding of mathematics. The author tells a series of short stories based on a group of people and their experiences living in her small town. One common theme among the stories is that they all involve mathematics. After reading the stories, a series of questions guides the reader to solve the problems. Mathematical topics such as square roots, finding percents, reading statistics, and more are covered in this engaging activity book.

Super One-Page Math Comics by Matt Friedman
Scholastic, 2002

This activity book presents a series of action-hero comic-book-style stories with follow-up activities to assist the superheroes in saving the day. The activities blend story elements, humor, and action, so that students do not feel as though they are working through a textbook set of activities. This activity book deftly blends students' love of reading comic books with practice in mathematical skills.

Unfolding Mathematics with Unit Origami by Betsy Franco and Diane Varner
Key Curriculum Press, 1999

This activity book is targeted specifically for high school algebra and geometry students. With sixteen activities, students are able to create three-dimensional origami models. Each activity increases in difficulty in both the design of the model and the mathematical concepts. Some mathematical concepts included are angle relationships and types of symmetry. Additionally, information on the art of origami and the masters of the craft are included throughout the book to combine a cross-curriculum experience between art and mathematics.

Reference Books

Classroom libraries generally have plenty of reference materials to support student learning. Reference books are an excellent way to provide students with a source of information when they are struggling with a particular concept and the textbook offers too little support.

We have a few favorites. *Math Dictionary: The Easy, Simple, Fun Guide to Help Math Phobics Become Math Lovers* (Monroe, 2006) is everything the title implies, and it includes helpful visual aids for readers. The *Dr. Math* series is extremely popular and covers mathematical subjects such as algebra (Math Forum Drexel University & Wolk-Stanley, 2003) and geometry (Math Forum Drexel University & Wolk-Stanley, 2004). The books' question-and-answer style, cartoon drawings, connections to everyday life, and Internet links make these books user-friendly and an asset to the math classroom.

A recent sensation in mathematical reference books are actress Danica McKellar's *Math Doesn't Suck* (2007), *Kiss My Math* (2008), and *Hot X: Algebra Exposed* (2010). Intended for girls, these books demystify mathematical understanding, while making analogies to food, shoes, dating, and even purchasing items on the popular online auction site eBay. Each chapter gives a straightforward approach to explaining concepts such as fractions and mixed numbers, prime factorization, rates and unit rates, and solving for x.

Concept Books

There are a wide variety of nonfiction styles and formats. Concept books are the most common, where the entire content of the book revolves around a particular topic or theme and is written to inform, yet hold the reader's interest. For example, in *The Joy of Pi* (1997), author David Blatner provides a historical framework for the world's most famous transcendental number, discussing why that number is so important, examining the Greek symbol representing pi, and including tricks to memorize the digits of pi. *The Joy of Pi* is the perfect example of a concept book augmenting a mathematical textbook, because it conveys essential information but does so in an inviting style. The book is filled with illustrations, quotations, and a running list of trivia about pi.

Fermat's Enigma: The Epic Quest to Solve The World's Greatest Mathematical Problem (Singh, 1997) is a fascinating concept book focusing on the mathematical proofs we take for granted. For example, an even number is always divisible by two. Mathematicians spend countless months and often years proving these statements. With in-depth descriptions of mathematical principles such as infinity, the Pythagorean theorem, and axioms of arithmetic, this concept book guides readers through complex mathematics and provides insight into the world of proofs. Readings like these make a perfect companion to the studying of a variety of proofs, grounding students' mathematical understanding with knowledge about their history and the mathematicians who worked so hard to make this knowledge possible.

Concept books like *The Joy of Pi* and *Fermat's Enigma* should be a staple in the classroom. Short sections can be used to augment the use of the textbook, especially because some concept books can be seen as interdisciplinary, straddling the line between math and other content areas. For example, *Just the Right Size: Why Big Animals Are Big and Little Animals Are Little* (Davies, 2009) takes an important scientific concept that governs the size that animals can grow and views it from a mathematical perspective. Simplified illustrations show how doubling the size of a three-dimensional object actually quadruples its surface area and increases its volume by a factor of eight. Young scientists will learn to draw mathematical conclusions as to why, for example, humans can't fly or walk on water using proportions, surface area, and volume.

Another example, *The Case of the Mummified Pigs and Other Mysteries in Nature* (Quinlan, 1995), draws on the popular fascination with crime scene investigation (CSI) mysteries and moves into the natural world. Some topics discuss disappearances of entire reindeer populations, sporadic hare infestations, unappetizing butterflies, and other mysteries in nature.

Mathematics can be pulled from each story to include limiting values, population models, and the design of statistical experiments. The interdisciplinary angle found in many concept books can be used to appeal to students with many different interests. Here are more of our favorite concept books for use in the mathematics classroom.

Career Ideas for Kids Who Like Math by Diane Lindsey Reeves
Illustrated by Nancy Bond
Facts on File, 2000

This is a middle grades concept book featuring career options for students who have a fondness for mathematics. Readers first take a self-interest test to help them navigate the fifteen highlighted careers, including urban planners, bankers, traffic planners, and computer consultants. Short biographies and job descriptions are included for each career. A follow-up book was published in 2007: *Career Ideas for Kids Who Like Math and Money*.

The Coast Mappers by Taylor Morrison
Houghton Mifflin Books, 2004

Long before GPS, maps, and satellites, sailors and travelers needed to know the shape of the coastline and sea floor. In the 1800s, this seemed like an impossible task. This true story follows Alexander Bache and George Davidson on their often-dangerous journey to map the Pacific coastline. The available methods to chart the coastline quickly evolved to include triangulation, angles, and other geometry. One section describes using protractors and theodolites to measure two angles of a triangle and solve for the third angle, which uses the theorem that all angles of a triangle will sum to 180 degrees. This historically significant work is also appropriate for the history classroom, providing opportunities for cross-curricular projects.

Go Figure! A Totally Cool Book About Numbers by Johnny Ball
DK Publishing, 2005

This trade book investigates interesting facts about numbers and math. Strange connections between the perimeter and area of a pyramid, the proportions in famous art, mathematical curves that are formed from cross-sections of a cone, and a brief history of famous mathematicians are just a few of the topics discussed. The short explanations and colorful pictures hold the reader's attention while providing a concise understanding of each topic. Short quizzes, matching games, and fun tricks are peppered throughout the pages. This book reads like an encyclopedia, so readers can choose to read it straight through or to flip to any page and learn something interesting about the numbers we take for granted.

Graphing Sports by Casey Rand
Heinemann-Raintree Books, 2010

From Heinemann-Raintree's *Real World Data* series, this book focuses on the data from a wide variety of sports including water polo, soccer, Olympic events, basketball, and football. In addition to facts, anecdotes, and descriptions of athletic wonders, this book serves as an excellent introduction to the fundamental methods of displaying quantitative and qualitative data. Bar graphs, pie charts, line graphs, pictographs, and tables are used to display and make sense of data related to each of the sporting events mentioned. Throughout the book, questions are posed to monitor reading comprehension and understanding of each graph, and readers are guided toward an in-depth and increasingly complex understanding of data representation.

The History of Counting by Denise Schmandt-Besserat
Morrow Junior Books, 1999

We often take our number system for granted. *The History of Counting* follows the evolution of our number system from the time when "one" and "many" were the only "numbers" to the infinite system we have today. The difficulty of using older systems, such as Roman numerals, for basic arithmetic is illustrated, giving readers a greater appreciation for today's base-10 number system. Other topics discussed include discrete and continuous numbers, natural numbers, divisibility, greatest common factors, and number prefixes. Illustrations soften the text on each page, and a glossary of terms provides further discussion of vocabulary in the text.

Mathematical Amazements and Surprises: Fascinating Figures and Noteworthy Numbers
by Alfred S. Posamentier and Ingmar Lehmann
Prometheus Books, 2009

This book is mathematical trivia at its best. Unusual relationships, shortcuts with mental arithmetic, and more are highlighted in this book by professors of mathematics. There is an entire chapter titled, "Mathematical Nuggets: Believe It-or-Not, but True". The introduction to the book explains, "this book is designed to open up the world of mathematical wonders through largely numerical and geometrical phenomena" (p. 7) and goes on to provide the example that the chances of finding two people with the same birth date in a room of thirty-five people is actually 80%. In addition to the oddities, this book also focuses on the beauty of mathematics, particularly geometry. The casual tone makes this an easy but enjoyable, and at times enlightening, read.

A Mathematical Nature Walk by John A. Adam
Princeton University Press, 2009

In a conversational style, Adams explores the connections between mathematics and the natural world, covering everything from rainbows to light and sound. Explore famous areas such as Loch Ness (How long will it take to empty?) and the Grand Canyon (How long will it take to fill with sand?). There is even a question about the possible existence of King Kong. Adams explains that the book generated from his love of walking and reflecting on everything from the shapes of meandering rivers to the path of intersecting waves. His book tells readers how to explore nature, science, and mathematics by taking a walk through their own neighborhoods.

A Mathematician Reads the Newspaper by John Allen Paulos
First Anchor Books, 1995

Paulos tackles the daily news using his keen mathematical perspective and cool logic, covering everything from advertising to the lottery to elections. Using short vignettes, Paulos uses a mathematical lens to analyze everything from politics to economics to sports across time periods. Easily adapted for classroom reading, this book will have students rethinking their perception of the news, even if it is entertainment news. Read his other works on mathematical literacy, including *Once Upon a Number: The Hidden Mathematical Logic of Stories* (1999) and *A Mathematician Plays the Stock Market* (2004).

Math Stuff by Theoni Pappas
Wide World Publishing, 2002

The introduction to this book explains quite clearly that this book is not about complicated equations or formulas. Instead, it is about everyday situations that involve mathematics, and some of those situations are unexpected. As author Pappas explains, most people "are unaware that deciding what to cook for dinner, which road to take at a fork, or prioritizing tasks are indeed forms of mathematical problem solving." Mathematics, she tells us, entails the discovery of patterns, "be they patterns in the shape of leaves or patterns of behavior" (p. x). Short sections and engaging topics make this an easy book to use for short reading activities. Our favorite section is called "Cricket Math," where Pappas explains that there is a connection between the weather's temperature and the chirp of a cricket, and that this relationship can be explored through a simple algebraic equation. Check out other works from Pappas, such as *The Joy of Mathematics* (1993) and *Mathematical Scandals* (1997).

Sacred Geometry by Miranda Lundy
Walker Publishing Company, 1998

Sacred Geometry pays homage to one of the oldest and most admired forms of mathematics: geometry. This book explains every aspect of geometry from the simplest definition. As readers move through the book, they are exposed to the fundamental relationships between a point, line, circle, sphere, ratios, and various two-dimensional and three-dimensional shapes that spawn from these more simplistic concepts. A similar book from Walker Publishing, *The Golden Section* (Olsen & Olsen, 2006), explores the golden ratio, Fibonacci numbers, and the mysterious relationships that occur in nature, art, and architecture.

Solving Crime with Numbers: The Numbers Behind Numb3rs by Keith Devlin and Gary Lorden
Penguin, 2007

In the pilot episode of the CBS television show *Numb3rs* (2005), mathematician Charlie Epps explains that he is "developing an application for the FBI . . . the problem involves finding an origin point from evidence provided by scattered effects," and it's this application that leads to the solution of the case.

Of course, Charlie Epps doesn't just offer viewers facts and logic; he has a certain finesse that not only makes for good television, but also makes mathematics cutting-edge. Further, Epps not only solves crimes with mathematics, he also explains mathematics through everyday analogies, which bridge content learning with prior knowledge. In the aforementioned episode, Epps uses the analogy of the water drops from a garden sprinkler to explain how his application works.

But does his math stand up in real life? Watch recordings of the episodes (or key scenes) while reading this book by Devlin and Lorden, the latter being the math consultant for the show, to find out.

Top Secret: A Handbook of Codes, Ciphers and Secret Writing by Paul B. Janeczko
Candlewick Press, 2004

This book introduces readers to the secret world of codes and ciphers. Several codes are examined and explained, such as hobo, dictionary, and Morse codes. Readers are shown how to create their own codes, as well as how to break them. Several codes mentioned have roots in mathematics, such as the Greek Square Cipher, the Route Transposition Cipher, and the Line Cipher, which use coordinates and line segments to encode messages. Such code systems can be used to introduce students to the coordinate plane, naming points on a plane, and constructing line segments.

Why Pi? by Johnny Ball
DK Publishing, 2009

Ball teaches us that mathematics is crucial to everything, particularly because we use it to measure things that are integral to every facet of our lives. Ball talks about using mathematics in the ancient world, famous mathematicians (who could sometimes be considered mathmagicians), and modern ways of measuring. He explores topics from the art of building aqueducts to mapping the world to the speed of light. Each chapter is broken down into short textboxes, and beautiful images and illustrations are included that are sure to capture the attention of any student.

Wonders of Numbers: Adventures in Mathematics, Mind, and Meaning by Clifford A. Pickover
Oxford University Press, 2002

With a wide array of *wonders*, there should be something of interest for every student in this book. Our attention was grabbed with the first entry on the table of contents: The Alien IQ Test. But other topics such as cryptorunes, fractal horizons, and spiral symmetry got our attention too. Everything about the book is connected mathematically in unique and interesting ways, including the dedication of the book: *To the apocalyptic magic square*. The book's introduction reminds us that with mathematics, integers in particular, we can "transcend space and time" and that "numbers will be our first means of communication with intelligent alien races" (p. x). Intrigued yet? Read on!

Biographies

Young adults are often seen reading biographies of rock stars, actresses, and athletes, but a biography of a mathematician, scientist, or even a politician can make for a fascinating read. Further, there is more variety in this genre of nonfiction than many people realize. Not all biographies are written chronologically or even about people.

Take, for example, *Zero: The Biography of a Dangerous Idea* (Seife, 2000) or *e: The Story of a Number* (Maor, 1994). Each of these alternative biographies follows the acceptance and discovery of undiscovered numbers. Along the way, readers are swept into a love affair with the intricacy and, sometimes, the simplicity of mathematics, as it breaks down important problems into sequential steps working toward a solution. Topics discussed in the aforementioned texts include place value, number theory, rules of exponents, principles of 0 and infinity, formation of logarithms, derivatives, and limits. Excerpts from these biographies, and others, can be used and applied to a wide variety of mathematics competencies.

In our research for this book, we found a dearth of biographies of mathematicians who worked outside the Western world. Recent scholarship has resulted in increased recognition for female mathematicians, but the lives of mathematicians who lived and worked in Asia, Africa, and South America are in short supply. (Perhaps the authors of this book will seek to remedy that lack.)

Historical books that highlight the obvious contributions of mathematicians from the Middle East—algebra derives from an Arabic word—can be found. Two of these histories are *The House of Wisdom: How Arabic Science Saved Ancient Knowledge and Gave Us the Renaissance* by Jim al-Khalili (2010) and *The House of Wisdom: How the Arabs Transformed Western Civilization* by Jonathan Lyons (2010). For a book that visually represents the diversity of mathematicians, see *Mathematicians: An Outer View of the Inner World* by Mariana Cook and Robert Clifford Gunning (2009), a collection of photographs of mathematicians accompanied by their autobiographical notes. And for a biography focusing on one man of African descent, try *Benjamin Banneker: Astronomer and Mathematician* by Allison Lassieur (2006).

Compilations of short biographies can enhance the study of mathematics and provide students with connections to the unit of study, while providing manageable chunks of text suitable for limited classroom time. *Mathematicians Are People, Too* (Reimer & Reimer, 1990) includes short biographies of mathematicians such as Archimedes, John Napier, Blaise Pascal, Sophie Germain, and Emmy Noether. Among the authors' stated goals is that students will learn that "mathematics has intrigued both men and women from all cultures" (p. iv). This book includes topics such as problem solving, geometry, algebra, estimation, measurement, and mathematical symbols.

Another compilation of biographies also focuses on women: *Women and Numbers: Lives of Women Mathematicians* (Perl, 1993). Biographies are included for Ada Lovelace, Mary Everett Boole, and even author Theoni Pappas, whose books are recommended in this chapter. Each featured woman has standard biographical information, accompanied by activities that connect with the mathematics represented.

Profiles in Mathematics is a great series of biographies through Morgan Reynolds Publishing for the math classroom, with books focusing on Alan Turing, René Descartes, Carl Friedrich Gauss, Sophie Germain, Pierre de Fermat, as well as a collection of ancient mathematicians and women mathematicians. This series takes a deeper look at famous mathematicians and highlights the circumstances of their lives that brought them to their most famous discoveries. Short, well-organized chapters are easy to read and provide breaks with side notes, pictures, and related textboxes. Mathematics shares the spotlight with biographical information, but it is peppered throughout each and every chapter. For example, when describing Descartes' interests in college, a textbox introduces Euclid's Elements. Other mathematical topics discussed in Descartes' biography include prime numbers, axioms of mathematics, the coordinate system, equations of a line, and definitions of geometric vocabulary (Gimbel, 2008).

Sophie Germain's biography (Ornes, 2008) is an interesting portrait of a true pioneer. In her time, it was not acceptable for women to practice mathematics and higher academics. To overcome these barriers, Germain began studying mathematics under a false name, and it was only later that she was able to openly pursue her work. One of her primary correspondents was Carl Friedrich Gauss. Germain's often-overlooked contributions to her field are chronicled in detail in this text. Topics related to Germain's work are discussed, including Fermat's Last Theorem, Diophantine equations, prime numbers, and graphical solutions of equations. This biography weaves mathematics throughout the story of how one woman overcame adversity to become very influential in her chosen field, applied mathematics.

As a worthy successor to the story of Sophie Germain, read *In Code: A Mathematical Journey* (Flannery & Flannery, 2002), the autobiography of Sarah Flannery who at 16 made headlines by creating an innovative encryption system. Puzzles are scattered throughout the book to provide examples of the mathematics of encryption.

USING TECHNOLOGY TO EXPLORE OTHER NONFICTION FORMATS

Text options need not be limited to books. There is a wealth of informational text that is readily available for teachers to use in various forms like magazines, websites, and blogs, and this informational text is increasingly found on the World-Wide Web. The immediacy of blogs is very appealing to young adults, and for this reason, we've chosen the weblog format to feature in this section.

Blogs are the precision machines of the publishing world. They can turn on a dime, responding to current events within seconds. Web-savvy consumers of news and opinion seek out bloggers who cover their areas of interest, which can be highly specific. This ability to cover a niche topic with pinpoint accuracy earns the best bloggers their audiences. And the best bloggers take advantage of something that journalistic tradition denies most reporters: the opportunity to develop a strong personal voice.

From the perspective of an educator wanting to foster students' writing ability, blogs are an interesting adjunct to more traditional reading. Adults now need to be able to adjust their writing voices to the media at hand. A business letter remains a formal piece of writing, but text messages use a markedly different and more informal style, and email occupies yet another spot on the formality continuum. The question of writing style is as important to mathematicians as it is to other professionals; a journal article would not be written in the same style as an interdepartmental memorandum or a job application letter. A savvy teacher will take every opportunity to make students aware of these nuances, and the best bloggers are all about nuance.

The following box by Brent Yorgey provides an example of a blogger's voice and of the blog's ability, as a medium, to allow a writer to concentrate on a very specific subject of particular interest to a niche readership like students of mathematics. We chose his blog to highlight due to his special interest in the beauty of mathematics. This book on the interrelationship of mathematics and literature seems to us to be the right place to celebrate art and beauty in mathematics.

One Blogger's Perception of the Beauty of Math

by Brent Yorgey

Take a blank sheet of paper and write the fraction 1/1 at the top. Now follow this simple rule: Whenever you have the fraction a/b, put $a/(a + b)$ below it to the left, and $(a + b)/b$ below to the right. Carrying out this process for 1/1 yields 1/2 and 2/1; carrying out the process for 1/2 and 2/1 in turn yields 1/3, 3/2, 2/3, and 3/1 in a third row across the page; and so on. This process defines an infinite tree of rational numbers called the *Calkin-Wilf tree*, named for Neil Calkin and Herbert Wilf, who introduced it in a short expository paper in 2000.

Although simple to define, the Calkin-Wilf tree has a number of amazing properties: For example, every positive rational number occurs somewhere in the tree, exactly once, in lowest terms. Listing the rationals in the tree row by row, from left to right, yields a list of all the positive rational numbers (1/1, 1/2, 2/1, 1/3, 3/2, . . .) in which every number has the same denominator as the numerator of the next, each number can be computed by a simple formula involving only the previous one, and the sequence of numerators has surprising connections to other areas of mathematics. It is an incredibly beautiful mathematical object, yielding new insight with each new point of view.

One might think that understanding and proving things about an object with such amazing properties, discovered only 10 years ago, must require very sophisticated mathematics. Nothing could be further from the truth! Beginning in December 2007 and continuing through October 2009, I wrote a ten-part series of blog posts (http://www.mathlesstraveled.com/?p=94) exploring the Calkin-Wilf tree and its properties. I tried to make the series accessible even to motivated middle school students, and it generated quite a bit of interest from students, educators, and armchair mathematics enthusiasts alike. I recently also had the opportunity to put my claims of accessibility to the test, when I presented the tree to the math club at a local middle school. Over the course of two separate 1-hour sessions (the second at their request), they happily explored the properties of the tree, discovering many for themselves—including some I hadn't thought of!—with only a bit of guidance from me.

Sharing knowledge with others is commendable; sharing insight is even better. But as I've learned, nothing compares to sharing your excitement and awe over something beautiful. This is what I strive to do every time I write and every time I teach. Our beautiful subject deserves nothing less!

A quick Internet search will yield many, many educational blogs. Here, we highlight some of our favorite blogs that feature mathematical themes. We have chosen sites that have an established history, but be aware that the World-Wide Web changes at the speed of light—literally. If you find that one of these blogs is no longer current, a quick web search will uncover others, because there are always people with something to say who will jump at the chance of using the Internet to broadcast their viewpoint.

And a final cautionary note—we have read multiple entries on each of these blogs and encountered no content unsuitable for the middle and high school students targeted by this book. Yet the nature of blogs is such that new material goes up every day. We cannot guarantee the content of tomorrow's post. Be familiar with your school's Internet policy in order to develop your own best policy for classroom Internet usage.

ANNOTATED BIBLIOGRAPHY OF MATHEMATICAL BLOGS

Dr. Steven Strogatz's entries to the *New York Times* Opinionator Blog
http://opinionator.blogs.nytimes.com/category/steven-strogatz

The beauty of the Internet is its ability to disseminate information to the entire world—and to do it in a way that can be accessed forever. While some blogs are open-ended, the format can also be used to present a self-contained series of articles like these by Steven Strogatz. Dr. Strogatz, a professor of applied mathematics at Cornell University, is the recipient of the Communications Award, a lifetime achievement award for the communication of mathematics to the general public. Thanks to the World-Wide Web, his series of ruminations on mathematical topics, originally posted between January and May 2010, remains available on the *New York Times* website.

Mathematics News, ScienceDaily's *Mathematics Blog*
http://www.sciencedaily.com/news/computers_math/mathematics

This blog presents summaries of recent mathematics-related news stories, including links to the original articles. Teachers will find material in these articles to enrich classroom discussion or to assign to secondary school students as independent reading. For example, a recent article at the time of this writing was "Using Science to Identify True Soccer Stars" (http://www.sciencedaily.com/releases/2010/06/100616171637.htm, 2010), a topic of obvious interest to students who may be reluctant math learners but who love athletics.

Math Moments, David Schwartz
http://davidschwartz.com/

David Schwartz is the author of almost 50 books about math including the popular picture books *G Is for Googol* (1998) and *On Beyond a Million* (1999). His website showcases his books and enthusiasm for mathematics in everyday life and includes his blog, which combines information about mathematics, writing, and research. In addition, his blog-style *Math Moments* is a collection of stories from students and families about the ways they encounter mathematics in their everyday lives. Schwartz takes each math moment and empowers readers to incorporate math in every tiny way possible. These blog entries can be used to open each math class and help students make the real-world connections they so often struggle to find. Teachers could even create their own classroom math moments, based on student stories of instances when they saw math in their own lives.

The Math Less Traveled: Explorations in Mathematical Beauty, Brent Yorgey
http://www.mathlesstraveled.com

An appreciation of the beauty and elegance of mathematics will stir a passion for the subject in students that can last a lifetime. Brent Yorgey has created this site, dedicated to that beauty and elegance. In Yorgey's words, "Math is about much more than figuring out when two trains will meet or calculating compound interest. Mathematics—like the hard sciences, but even more so—seeks to discover and understand the deep, elegant structure built into the very fabric of the universe. And it's no surprise, really, that the deep mathematical structure of a universe featuring such things as clouds, crystal lattices, rainbows, galaxies, and atoms turns out to be beautiful."

Mister Teacher, Jamie Tubbs
http://www.misterteacher.blogspot.com

There are many wonderful blogs created by working math teachers, and we invite you to explore that vast world, but we can only pick a few blogs for inclusion here. *Mister Teacher*, created in 2002 by Jamie Tubbs, was selected because it embraces new technology as a teaching tool, a concept that was partially responsible for the creation of the book in your hands. At the time of this writing, recent posts included the classroom use of a computer game, as well as a listing of applications for smart phones. Other creative uses of technology offered at *Mister Teacher* include mini-movies, offered free of charge, that can be downloaded and displayed on smartboards in the classroom.

NONFICTION IN THE MATH CLASSROOM

At the close of this chapter, we have presented two lesson plans that blend literacy skills obtained from reading and interpreting nonfiction with the mathematical skills implicit in the material being read. "Grappling over Grades" brings home a real-life situation for most students: How are test scores earned over a term, a semester, or a school year boiled down to a single grade? What does "average" mean, anyway? In the second lesson plan, the story of Archimedes ties literacy and mathematics to the study of history, providing a particularly rich learning experience. We think your students will enjoy these.

LESSON PLAN 4-1

"GRAPPLING OVER GRADES" ANTICIPATION GUIDE

In anticipation guides, questions are given before a reading assignment. These questions are geared toward preteaching concepts or vocabulary or toward opening discussion for further instruction on a concept. Prereading activities like anticipation guides are often paired with a postreading activity, so that students can practice concepts, revisit their original answers, and possibly form new opinions.

(Continued)

LESSON PLAN 4-1 (Continued)

Materials: "Grappling over Grades" story from the *40 Fabulous Math Mysteries Kids Can't Resist* activity book (Lee & Miller, 2001), pre- and postreading worksheet

Duration: 40 minutes: 15 minutes prereading and discussion, 10 minutes reading, 15 minutes postreading and discussion

Applicable Common Core Standards:

Chapter 6: Statistics and Probability

Chapter 7: Statistics and Probability

High School:

Statistics and Probability: Interpreting Categorical and Quantitative Data
   Making Inferences and Justifying Conclusions

Procedure: By the time they read this passage, students should know the difference between measures of central tendency (mean, median, and mode), or "averages," but may not yet understand why the word "average" is not appropriate to use. Hand out the worksheet, printed with the prereading questions on one side and the postreading questions on the other. Instruct students to complete only the prereading side. You may choose for this to be done in a small group setting or individually. Spend about 10 minutes discussing answers, but do not give any hints as to which responses are more favorable.

Pass out the "Grappling over Grades" story, which describes a disagreement between a student and a teacher who claim to have a different "average" for the student's grade. As the narrator investigates the discrepancy, the actual grades are given.

Instruct students to flip over their worksheet and complete the postreading questions. In doing this, students will realize that the teacher and student in the story both have a correct "average," but one is more appropriate (or commonly used) when giving class grades. Reserve some time after the activity to discuss situations when the different types of "averages" are more appropriate than others and to explore how students' responses to the prereading questions changed after reading the passage. Through the two sets of questions and discussion, students will be able to formulate their own ideas about the word "average" and, in turn, develop an understanding of why mathematics uses more descriptive words such as mean, median, and mode.

"Grappling Over Grades" Pre- and Postreading Questions
Prereading Questions

1. What is the definition of the word "average" in statistics?

_____

_____

2. Is it possible to have more than one "average"? Explain.

_____

_____

3. What are the mean, median, and mode for a set of numbers?

_____

_____

Postreading Questions

4. Put Lucia's test scores in order from least to greatest.

_____

_____

5. Find the mean, median, and mode of her test scores. Show your work.

_____

_____

6. Why did Lucia and Mrs. Lopez have different "averages"? Was either person wrong?

_____

_____

_____

7. Look at your answer to Question 2. If you can provide a better answer after reading the story, do so here.

_____

_____

8. When is it appropriate to use each kind of "average"?

_____

_____

Modifications for High School: This activity serves as an introduction for middle school students on appropriate measures of central tendency, but the topic can be extended to include high school audiences by having them find the measures for a similar sample. High school students can then use the Normal Distribution Model to discuss locations of the two grades and how they fit the Empirical Rule in statistics.

LESSON PLAN 4-2

ARCHIMEDES R.A.F.T.

The acronym for this activity—R.A.F.T.—stands for Role, Audience, Form, and Topic. R.A.F.T. addresses more complex concepts particularly well, because comprehension is extended through writing. Students are asked to provide four pieces of information, based on their reading. The Role is the position or voice taken by the writer of the passage being studied. The Audience is the group of people whom the writer is addressing. The Form defines the type of writing, which can vary from a letter to a wanted ad to a poem. The Topic, while stemming from the overall topic of the reading, is further narrowed, based on the selections in an option chart provided to the students. The option chart should include a variety of forms and styles, and it should range from literal to abstract, so that all students connect with some element of the reading passage.

Materials: *Archimedes* (Gow 2005)
Duration: 80 minutes: 30 minutes reading, 50 minutes writing

Applicable Common Core Standards:

Grade 7: Geometry

Grade 8: Geometry

High School:

Modeling

Geometry: Circles

   Expressing Geometric Properties with Equations

   Geometric Measurement and Dimension

   Modeling with Geometry

Procedure: Assign chapters in the book *Archimedes* that deal with surface area, cylinders, or spheres for students to read during class or for homework. You should preread the text so you can assign chapters based on your class's mathematical and reading levels: Some chapters will serve well as a review of concepts dealing with three-dimensional objects, whereas some provide an extension on concepts.

Once students have completed their assigned reading, allow them to choose a Role, Audience, Format, and Topic from the list shown below. You may allow students to create their own R.A.F.T., as long as you confirm the relevance and mathematical value of their suggestion.

Once the topics are determined, students will spend a specified period of time, usually a single class period, to write a brief paper in four parts—Role, Audience, Format, and Topic. Provide short-term goals throughout the class period for students to have portions of their assignments completed, such as brainstorming, introduction, and final draft. Pacing this assignment will give students extra support to have a complete product by the end of the class period.

Emphasize to the students that the goal of the assignment is to show their understanding of the mathematics. While creativity is a nice contribution, it is not the reason for the assignment. Upon completion of the R.A.F.T., students will have demonstrated their various understandings of surface area and three-dimensional figures in a different way from the modes traditionally used in mathematics classes, such as problem solving and testing.

Role	Audience	Format	Topic
Archimedes	Greeks	Summary of your book	The relationship between a circle's diameter and circumference and why it is important
Archimedes	Math students of the future	Letter in a time capsule	Why does knowing the area of a circle help in identifying the area of polygons?
Math student	Archimedes	Letter	How did you use Archimedes' idea of polygons inside and outside of a circle to calculate the value of pi?
Dositheus	Journal	Journal entry	How did Archimedes teach you to calculate the surface area of a sphere?
Archimedes	His son	Dialogue	What did you learn about spheres?
A cylinder	A sphere	Invitation to a family reunion	How are circles and spheres related? Why sphere should come to the family reunion

(Continued)

LESSON PLAN 4-2 (Continued)

Role	Audience	Format	Topic
Plutarch	Greeks	Obituary	What contributions Archimedes makes to mathematics
College scout	Potential students	Brochure	Why someone should consider coming to Alexandria to study geometry

References

Gow, M. (2005). *Archimedes: Mathematical Genius of the Ancient World*. Berkeley Heights, NJ: Enslow Publishers.

al-Khalili, J. (2011). *The house of wisdom: How Arabic science saved ancient knowledge and gave us the Renaissance*. New York: Penguin.

Blatner, D. (1997). *The joy of pi*. New York: Walker & Company.

Common Core State Standards Initiative. (2010). *Common Core State Standards for English language arts & literacy in history/social studies, science, and technical subjects*. Washington, DC: National Governors Association Center for Best Practices and the Council of Chief State School Officers.

Cook, M., & Gunning, R. (2009). *Mathematicians: An outer view of the inner world*. Princeton, NJ: Princeton University Press.

Davies, N. (2009). *Just the right size: Why big animals are big and little animals are little*. Somerville, MA: Candlewick.

Flannery, S., & Flannery, D. (2001). *In code: A mathematical journey*. Chapel Hill, NC: Algonquin Books.

Gimbel, S. (2008). *Profiles in mathematics: Rene Descartes*. Greensboro, NC: Morgan Reynolds Publishing.

Lassieur, A. (2006). *Benjamin Banneker: Astronomer and mathematician*. Mankato, MN: Capstone Press.

Lee, M., & Miller, M. (2001). *40 fabulous math mysteries kids can't resist*. New York: Scholastic.

Lombardo, M. A. (2003). *Mastering math through magic*. Columbus, OH: Linworth Publishing.

Lyons, J. (2010). *The house of wisdom: How the Arabs transformed western civilization*. New York: Bloomsbury Press.

Maor, E. (1994). *e: The story of a number*. Princeton, NJ: Princeton University Press.

Math Forum Drexel University, & Wolk-Stanley, J. (2003). *Dr. Math gets you ready for algebra: Learning pre-algebra is easy*. New York: John Wiley & Sons, Inc.

Math Forum Drexel University, & Wolk-Stanley, J. (2004). *Dr. Math introduces geometry: Learning geometry is easy! Just ask Dr. Math!* New York: John Wiley & Sons, Inc.

McKellar, D. (2007). *Math doesn't suck: How to survive middle school math without losing your mind or breaking a nail*. New York: Hudson Street Press.

McKellar, D. (2008). *Kiss my math: Showing pre-algebra who's boss*. New York: Hudson Street Press.

McKellar, D. (2010). *Hot X: Algebra exposed*. New York: Hudson Street Press.

Monroe, E. E. (2006). *Math dictionary: The easy, simple, fun guide to help math phobics become math lovers*. Honesdale, PA: Boyds Mill Press.

Olsen, S., & Olsen, S. (2006). *The golden section*. New York: Walker & Company.

Ornes, S. (2008). *Profiles in mathematics: Sophie Germain*. Greensboro, NC: Morgan Reynolds Publishing.

Perl, T. (1993). *Women and numbers: Lives of women mathematicians*. San Carlos, CA: Wide World Publishing.

Quinlan, S. E. (1995). *The case of the mummified pigs and other mysteries in nature*. Honesdale, PA: Boyds Mill Press.

Reimer, L., & Reimer, W. (1990). *Mathematicians are people, too: Stories from the lives of great mathematicians*. Parsippany, NJ: Dale Seymour Publications.

Schwartz, D. (1998). *G is for googol*. New York: Scholastic.

Schwartz, D. (1999). *On beyond a million*. New York: Scholastic.

Seife, C. (2000). *Zero: The biography of a dangerous idea*. New York: Penguin Group.

Singh, S. (1997). *Fermat's enigma: The epic quest to solve the world's greatest mathematical problem*. New York: Anchor Books.

Chapter 5

Picture Books: Where Math, Text, and Illustrations Collide

With contributions by Megan Stein

INTRODUCTION

Picture books are often misunderstood or perceived as merely books for young children, but picture books are not necessarily written at any specific level. They are simply a format for presenting text, stories, and ideas that can take on any genre, style, and level. In fact, picture books can be an excellent vehicle for learning content, like mathematics, in surprising ways. *A Mirror to Nature* (Yolen, 2009) is a compilation of short poems that reference photographs of animals in their natural habitats, illustrating reflection and the resulting lines of horizontal symmetry. See Lesson Plan 2-1 at the end of Chapter 2 for an anticipation guide that takes advantage of the visual input from these photographs.

Steven Pinker, a prominent linguist, said reading Dr. Seuss's *The Cat in the Hat Comes Back* (1958), "forced me to think about nested sets, infinitesimals, Zeno's paradox, and other concepts that I studied much later in mathematics" (Silvey, 2009, p. 147). Perhaps it is the imagination of the story, the flow and style of the writing, or the complexity of the illustrations, but Pinker found sophisticated mathematical allusions in that one Dr. Seuss picture book.

Because picture books are a format and not a level, there are many subgenres and styles. Widely recognized picture book types are ABC and counting books, which can range in audience from young children to adults depending on the topics addressed. ABC books focus on a particular topic that is then represented with each letter of the alphabet followed by an appropriate illustration. *G Is for Googol* (Schwartz, 1998) is a complex ABC book illustrating topics such as B is for Binary (p. 6), R is for Rhombicosidodecahedron (p. 37), and T is for Tessellate (p. 41).

Counting books are similar in style and do help reinforce the learning of basic numbers for young children, but more sophisticated counting books are available that deliver more sophisticated concepts than one, two, or three. For example, *Anno's Mysterious Multiplying Jar* (Anno, 1983) expands on the traditional counting book to explore the concept of factorials. The illustrations walk the reader through solving the story's culminating word problem. Other types of picture books can include concept (or informational) books and storybooks. Concept books represent informational content, such as *On Beyond a Million* (Schwartz, 1999), which explores place values of large numbers and their equivalent exponential representations with whimsical illustrations, making learning these middle school concepts easy.

Storybooks are the most popular type of picture book and are often the winners of the American Library Association's Caldecott Award for excellence in picture book illustrations. Picture storybooks for young adults should tell a compelling or interesting story appropriate for the older student that is enhanced by the illustrations. In other words, the best picture storybooks present stories that could not be told—or, at least, could not be told as well—without the pictures.

In the following box, Cindy Neuschwander talks about her extremely popular and complex picture storybook series about a knight named Sir Cumference and his quests to discover the properties of circles, angles, three-dimensional shapes, and more. This clever series uses puns on traditional mathematical vocabulary to create unique characters and situations. For example, when Sir Cumference is turned into the Dragon of Pi, his son, Radius, must find the correct dose of medication, which

---

Sir Cumference

by Cindy Neuschwander

As a practicing teacher and writer, I have found that math literature is an effective tool for presenting mathematical concepts to students. Everyone loves a good story. It is memorable and enjoyable.

When I write my stories, I remember something I learned many years ago. Dr. Calvin Irons, a math educator working in Australia, suggested that every student of mathematics should pass through four distinct stages of mathematical language development to gain comprehension of new concepts. These stages are explained here with examples based on *Sir Cumference and the Dragon of Pi* (1999):

1. *Natural Language:* This is the descriptive language that people use every day. For example, in the story, Radius first thinks about the idea of pi as he examines the crust of a real pie. Pies are something most people have had experience with.

2. *Language of Materials:* This is communicating a math concept with tangible materials. Radius thinks about the relationship between the circumference and the diameter by measuring round objects like a bowl and a wheel of cheese. Students can likewise use round objects or paper circles and string to think about this relationship.

3. *Language of Mathematics:* This means communicating using mathematical terms. Here, the idea of pi is expressed in the story by stating that there is a relationship between the diameter and the circumference of a circle. It is called pi. Pi means that approximately 3 and 1/7th diameters equal one circumference.

4. *Written Symbolic Language:* The final step is communicating with the abstract language of mathematical symbols, saying $\pi = c/D$.

All too often when I studied mathematics as a kid, teachers started instructing at the fourth and most complicated stage of mathematical language development. This left me scratching my head and "not getting it."

Math literature, at its best, incorporates all of Dr. Irons' levels, helping students get a grasp of the material they are trying to master, step by step. This progression takes students from the most concrete levels of thinking to the most abstract, doing it in a way that helps them to understand.

When I write my math stories, I am mindful of mathematical language development. I also work at layering the mathematics so that basic concepts are readily understandable and more complicated concepts are alluded to. In this way, students who are ready for more can take the stories to greater depths mathematically.

For example, in *Sir Cumference and the Isle of Immeter* (2006), I wrote about area and perimeter. But I also sprinkled in a few ideas about calculus. I named the sea serpent the Palimpsest with the hope that a few readers might be curious enough to read about Archimedes and the discovery of his writings on a reused medieval parchment.

I always hope my stories are fun to read, mathematically sound, and memorable. Enjoy them and the math!

turns out to be the relationship of the distance through the center of the circle and around—a very familiar ratio, indeed, to students of mathematics.

The most important characteristic of picture books is that they blend two media in order to tell a story or relay content: text and illustrations. We know that this format is important for older readers, particularly young adult boys, who devour a medium that uses a similar blending: comic books. The blending, though, implies that the illustrations do more than just represent the story or content. Instead, the illustrations extend and enhance the story or content.

In *The Lion's Share* (McElligott, 2009), the illustrations teach readers about fractions through visual representations and also provide closure to the story not found in the text alone. As with other picture books, the visual nature of this wonderful narration of fractions can appeal to visual learners and to students who are struggling readers. *The Lion's Share* also provides an opportunity for hands-on classroom activities that take advantage of its straightforward storyline.

In the following box, author Sarah C. Campbell discusses the photographs that are pivotal in her picture book, *Growing Patterns: Fibonacci Numbers in Nature* (2010).

Activity: Sketching (or Eating) Your Way Through the Text with *The Lion's Share*

by Matthew McElligott

Applicable Common Core Standards

Grade 6: Ratios and Proportional Relationships

High School:

Functions: Linear, Quadratic, and Exponential Models

Modeling

Conflict ensues when the Lion's first guest takes half of the cake. The turmoil increases with each page when each animal at the Lion's dinner party takes half of the remaining cake. How will this end?

After your class has enjoyed the book and learned the cake's fate, make the drama of the story more tangible by having students draw area models of the remaining cake. Make the drama more tangible (and taste-able!) still by bringing in an actual cake to demonstrate the action in this book and to demonstrate how it is divided into successive fractions. For more advanced students, classroom discussion can include infinite series and even the concept of limits in calculus.

The significant difference in mathematical sophistication between fractions and series and limits illustrates the potential in developing lesson plans from stories and real-life incidents. Mathematical knowledge builds on itself, giving a creative teacher great scope in developing lessons.

Activity: Fibonacci Numbers in Nature

by Sarah Campbell

When I decided to write a picture book about Fibonacci numbers, I knew I wanted to illustrate the book with photographs. Initially, I tried a very simple layout. Each page had a single photograph paired with a block of text. With that approach, neither the text nor the layout seemed to be working. I had taken pictures of as many natural examples of Fibonacci numbers as I could find: flowers, fruit, vegetables, pinecones, pineapples, and the nautilus shell. After a basic explanation of the pattern, the text ended up reading like a list. I knew it didn't work.

I went back to my research. The visual that I kept being drawn to was the set of nested squares that some writers called a Fibonacci grid. I made my own grids, first out of construction paper and then fabric. What I really liked about the grid was that it served as a bridge for me from the simple number pattern (1, 1, 2, 3, 5, 8, . . .) to the Fibonacci spiral. I started playing around with a layout that would start with a one-by-one square and build square by square to the entire grid. Each square would contain a photograph of a flower with the number of petals that matched the unit size of the square. I really liked the page turn near the end of the book that would go from a graphic of nested boxes with a drawn spiral to the image of the nautilus.

I sketched a quick storyboard and realized that having the visual build-up would help me give the story a narrative pull. I worked with the text and layout (including cutting out some photos and examples) until the story had three distinct sections: a section with photographs of flowers that illustrated the pattern; a section that introduced the idea of spirals going in opposite directions (such as pinecones and sunflowers); and a section about the Fibonacci spiral on the nautilus. This matched the progression of the complexity of the ideas presented in the book.

When I do a read aloud, I do a lot of pointing. I tap the petals as I count, and I trace my finger around the spirals. As a visual learner myself, I know that having photographs *and* a layout that support the concept of a growing pattern helps with comprehension. This multilayered approach also makes *Growing Patterns: Fibonacci Numbers in Nature* a book for many different reading levels and one that can be enjoyed more than once.

Because picture books are far shorter than novels or other nonfiction works, their inclusion in the classroom is much more manageable. Reading a novel together as a class may take a semester, but reading a picture book might take only one class period. Choosing the right picture books to use with middle and high school students does require a careful examination for appropriate content, storytelling that resonates with young adults, and illustrations that are appealing to this age group.

Their format, length, and overall appeal make picture books versatile in the mathematics classroom with many options for integrating books into instruction that goes far beyond merely reading a book aloud to the class. Interactive reading guides, vocabulary concept maps, double-entry journals, and other strategies discussed in previous chapters can be employed when integrating picture books into instruction.

As an example, we have provided a classroom activity investigating the various aspects of the work of Pythagoras in the activities at the end of this chapter.

The Once Upon a Time Map Book (Hennessy, 2004) is a travel guide for classic fairytale lands such as Wonderland and Oz, using conversion factors and coordinate geometry. The book serves as an activity itself. For example, in a tour of Neverland, readers are instructed to: "Moor your boat to Mermaid Cove (E1)" and "Go West 6 pirate miles" (p. 1). Important mathematical concepts can be enhanced through discussion and critical thinking. Teachers can begin discussions with questions such as, "Which symbol references the horizontal coordinate? Is this always the case?" Once students synthesize their knowledge and are able to articulate their thoughts, they have truly mastered the content.

What follows is an annotated bibliography of our favorite picture books with mathematical topics that are appropriate for middle and high school classrooms. We include elements of the story as well as the mathematics in each annotation.

ANNOTATED BIBLIOGRAPHY OF PICTURE BOOKS FOR MIDDLE AND HIGH SCHOOL MATH CLASSROOMS

A Place for Zero: A Math Adventure by Angeline Sparagna LoPresti
Illustrated by Phyllis Hornung
Charlesbridge Publishing, 2003

King Multiplus and Queen Addeline rule the country of Digitaria with their positive attitude, but one number in the country is very unhappy. All of the numbers One through Nine have jobs, except for Zero. One day, Count Infinity accidentally puts Zero and One into the numberator machine, which adds numbers together. They were all surprised when another One appears. Zero has finally found a job; he is the additive identity! It is not long before the king discovers many more uses for Zero: zero product property, place value holder, and more! Understanding these foundational concepts can lead students into a deeper understanding of mathematical operations.

A Very Improbable Story by Edward Einhorn
Illustrated by Adam Gustavson
Charlesbridge Publishing, 2008

Ethan wakes up the morning of his soccer game to find a cat on his head. But this cat is not his; it's a probability cat named Odds. The cat refuses to leave until Ethan wins one of Odds' probability games. The first game involves the probability of pulling matching socks out of Ethan's drawer. Ethan loses. It's not long before Ethan realizes probability is all around him, and it can even help him become a better soccer player. With Odds' help, Ethan gains an understanding of independent events, ratios, and predicting outcomes that helps him discover the best way to score a goal at his soccer game.

Beanstalk: The Measure of a Giant by Ann McCallum
Illustrated by James Balkovek
Charlesbridge Publishing, 2006

This is no ordinary take on the classic *Jack and the Beanstalk* story. One morning, Jack wakes up to a giant beanstalk growing outside his window. When he climbs to the top, he meets a giant boy named Ray. They get along instantly and spend most of their time trying to figure out ways to play together. Jack must use his understanding of measurement to figure out how to make games between the two boys fair, given the huge difference in their size. This spin on the classic children's tale makes ratios fun. Readers will gain an understanding of writing ratios or "Ray shows" (p. 31) to represent relationships, as well as using proportional relationships to find measurements. The book can easily translate into a classroom activity, creating games for the two friends using proportional relationships.

Count Me a Rhyme: Animal Poems by the Numbers by Jane Yolen
Photographs by Jason Stemple
Boyds Mill Publishing, 2006

Jane Yolen treats readers to beautiful photographs of wildlife accompanied by relevant, thoughtful poems highlighting numbers and nature. Each picture and poem combination focuses on a number from 1 to 10, using a multitude of vocabulary terms to represent each number. Prefixes, Roman numerals, and vocabulary for the first ten numbers are explored. This book makes an obvious correlation between math and vocabulary that is often undervalued.

Cut Down to Size at High Noon: A Math Adventure by Scott Sundby
Illustrated by Wayne Geehan
Charlesbridge Publishing, 2000

The citizens of the town of Cowlick are known for their creative hairstyles. Carriages, eagles, cows, and horses adorn the crowns of Cowlick folks' heads. The creator of such haircuts is French barber Louie Cutorze, but when Buzzsaw the barber blows into town, a haircutting duel is the only way to decide who stays and goes. To their surprise, the barbers end up with equally creative hairstyles. Upon Louie's head is a giant grasshopper, and on Buzzsaw's head is a mini-locomotive. The barbers teach each other the art of using scale drawings to make small things large and large things small. Detailed scale drawing illustrations help connect the mathematics to the story, and the book can easily translate into an activity creating a variety of images using scale drawings.

Growing Patterns: Fibonacci Numbers in Nature by Sarah C. Campbell
Photographs by Sarah C. Campbell and Richard P. Campbell
Boys Mill Publishing, 2010

Fibonacci numbers are a familiar mathematical concept, but do we really know what they are or where they can be found? *Growing Patterns* takes readers on a journey to discover these special numbers through crisp, spectacular photographs of nature such as flowers and fruit. Rather than giving explicit definitions up front, Campbell allows readers to discover the relationship between these numbers using arithmetic, visual, and verbal cues. Readers will be delighted to see the intricacy of Fibonacci numbers in plants and animals with vivid photographs that are clearly labeled to demonstrate the pattern in nature. As a bonus, the author includes a glossary and an informational page about the Fibonacci numbers, including the mathematician who made this sequence famous.

The Lion's Share: A Tale of Halving Cake and Eating It, Too by Matthew McElligott
Walker Publishing Company, 2009

A jungle tea party goes awry when each animal guest takes half of the remaining cake. When the smallest guest, the ant, takes her piece, there is a mere one two-hundred-fifty-sixth left of the cake. The book explores fractions of fractions and multiplication as well as the connection between halving and doubling numbers.

Minnie's Diner: A Multiplying Menu by Dayle Ann Dodds
Illustrated by John Manders
Candlewick Press, 2007

Papa McFay has ordered that Will, Bill, Phil, Gill, and Dill finish their chores on the farm before they can eat. It's not long before the tempting aromas from Minnie's Diner reach young Will McFay's nose. He can't resist, and he leaves his chores to order a special at Minnie's Diner. Soon to follow is brother Bill, who orders double what the brother before had. As each brother abandons his chores, Minnie's workload multiplies. The whimsical rhyming and anticipation of the increasing orders will entertain readers. The story lends itself to discussion of direct variation and recursive and explicit sequences.

Multiplying Menace: The Revenge of Rumpelstiltskin by Pam Calvert
Illustraded by Wayne Geehan
Charlesbridge Publishing, 2006

On Prince Peter's tenth birthday, he discovers that a new puppy is not his only birthday surprise: Rumpelstiltskin has returned to claim Peter in return for the services he provided the queen years ago! After Rumpelstiltskin wreaks havoc on the kingdom with his magic multiplying stick, Peter agrees to go with Rumpelstiltskin in hopes of finding a way to save his kingdom. Peter learns the magic of the multiplication sticks and discovers that "times a fraction leaves hardly any." Readers will enhance their understanding of multiplication with whole numbers and fractions, as well as gain insight into direct and inverse variation.

The Once Upon a Time Map Book by B. G. Hennessy
Illustrated by Peter Joyce
Candlewick Press, 1999

The Once Upon a Time Map Book guides readers through enchanted lands from classic fairy tales. Comprehensive instructions give readers tours of magical lands, such as Wonderland with Alice, Neverland with Peter Pan, and Oz with Dorothy. Each land is displayed on a traditional map that includes coordinates, legend entries, and scale factors to represent distances. Readers will find themselves using distances like *munchkin miles* and *white rabbit hops* to navigate toward specified coordinates. This book gives a lighthearted take on scale factors and coordinates that students will enjoy inside and outside of the classroom.

Pythagoras and the Ratios by Julie Ellis
Illustrated by Phyllis Hornung Peacock
Charlesbridge Publishing, 2010

Octavius wants to play in the next music contest, but the pipes that he made sound terrible! Pythagoras has a knack for figuring out how things work, and tries to fix Octavius' pipes by comparing them to his own. Pythagoras discovers that the relationships between the lengths of each pipe are very important to their sounds, and he uses the relationship to fix Octavius' pipes.

Soon his cousins, Reyna and Amara, come looking for someone to fix their lyres. The stringed instruments are quite different from pipes, and Pythagoras must use his understanding of relationships to fix them. Pythagoras and his cousins gain a valuable understanding of relationships and how they can be used in music to create melody. Readers will uncover the important mathematical concept of ratios and how they can be used outside of a classroom. As a bonus, the author includes historical information regarding Pythagorean ratios.

Rabbits, Rabbits Everywhere: A Fibonacci Tale by Ann McCallum
Illustrated by Gideon Kendall
Charlesbridge Publishing, 2007

The Pied Piper has already saved the town of Hamelin from rats, and now he lives in Chee. The people of Chee happily harvest food for the wizard, but one day, the greedy Pied Piper tells a "fibb" to the wizard that there is no food. To punish the people, the wizard releases two magical rabbits: "Fibb" and "Knot." Before long, there are so many rabbits that the people of Chee are miserable. A local girl named Amanda uses her wit and intellect to uncover the mysterious sequence of "Fibb" and "Knot." Amanda and the townsfolk learn a valuable lesson about fibbing and the sequence that occurs when Fibb and Knot of Chee are released on the town.

Sir Cumference Series
Sir Cumference and the First Round Table by Cindy Neuschwander and Wayne Geehan
Charlesbridge Publishing, 1997

Sir Cumference, Lady Di of Ameter, and Radius are introduced in this first picture book adventure by Cindy Neuschwander. It appears that the

Circumscribers, people from a neighboring village, are preparing to wage war on Sir Cumference's kingdom. All the knights rush to the king's castle and sit around his table to discuss what they will do, but the table is so long and rectangular that everyone must shout. Sir Cumference decides he will take the current table and transform it into a different shape.

He tries several shapes by cutting and rotating the current table, but there is always a problem. After whittling the table smaller and smaller into an oval, the knights realize a round table is the best solution, but they need a bigger one. Sir Cumference, Lady Di of Ameter, and Radius set off to find the right materials to create a round table, and in the process of saving the kingdom, the heroes discover the basic properties of a circle.

Subsequent books, *Sir Cumference and the Dragon of Pi* (1999) and *Sir Cumference and the Isle of Immeter* (2006), continue the investigation of circles, their properties, their relationships, and relevant vocabulary. Other books in the series include *Sir Cumference and the Great Knight of Angleland* (2001), which explores vocabulary and properties of geometry; *Sir Cumference and All the King's Tens* (2009), which explores place values and working with large numbers; and *Sir Cumference and the Sword in the Cone* (2003), which explores nets of three-dimensional figures and relationships that can be used to find surface area and volume.

What's Your Angle, Pythagoras? by Julie Ellis
Illustrated by Phyllis Hornung
Charlesbridge Publishing, 2004

What's Your Angle, Pythagoras? is described as a "math adventure." It follows young Pythagoras as he stumbles upon one of the most famous theorems in mathematics. The story is, of course, not historically accurate; however, making Pythagoras a clumsy, curious boy gives young adult readers a more approachable character. The proof for the Pythagorean theorem is woven into the story through pictures and narration, with a few examples and applications incorporated into the story to reinforce the concept to readers. Crisp illustrations by Phyllis Hornung do an excellent job of making the math visual.

This book proves that reading can be easy and fun, while still incorporating complex mathematical concepts.

THE UTILITY OF PICTURE BOOKS FOR STUDENTS AT ALL LEVELS OF MATHEMATICAL STUDY

As you will see when you review Lesson Plan 5-1, based on *What's Your Angle, Pythagoras?* this book covers some fairly sophisticated mathematics, including the Pythagorean theorem and some introductory trigonometry. We've specifically included this activity to highlight the potential uses of picture books with students who might ordinarily be considered too old for this format. Your students may find themselves surprised by the things they learn from a book that has pictures.

LESSON PLAN 5-1

WHAT'S YOUR ANGLE, PYTHAGORAS? READING GUIDE

A reading guide is a series of prompts and questions that divide large bodies of reading into smaller assignments and manageable-sized concepts. Questions require multiple levels of thinking. The ability to adequately answer the questions signals to readers that they have read the previous passage with complete comprehension. Reading guides are geared toward developing metacognitive skills.

Applicable Common Core Standards

Grade 8: Geometry

High School:

Geometry: Similarity, Right Triangles, and Trigonometry

Expressing Geometric Properties with Equations

Modeling with Geometry

Functions: Trigonometric Functions

Modeling

Materials: *What's Your Angle, Pythagoras?* (Ellis, 2004), reading guide worksheet

Duration: 50 minutes for grade level readers

Procedure: Hand out the reading guide to each student. Instruct students to answer the questions as they read the story. The story is divided into small portions or ideas, so that students are not overwhelmed with large amounts of reading. At the conclusion of each reading assignment, students have a question to answer based on the reading just completed. The progression and order of questions should naturally signal to students when they have missed a key concept and need to reread a portion of the story. This serves as a cognitive aid for struggling readers.

The featured book, *What's Your Angle, Pythagorus?* relies heavily on pictures to teach the proof of the Pythagorean theorem, so students should be given sufficient reading time to look at the pictures and explore their significance.

At the conclusion of the reading, students will have read and reflected on the Pythagorean theorem and its proof and applications. The guide and story serve as the primary teaching tools in this lesson; however, you may choose to discuss the theorem further or provide extra practice for homework.

What's Your Angle, Pythagoras? Reading Guide

Directions: Use this reading guide to navigate through the story. Answer the questions as you go.

1. Organize the following vocabulary words in the following categories. Most of these words should be in your notes, if you need help remembering what they mean.

   hypotenuse   leg   right triangle
   isosceles triangle   equilateral triangle   right angle

I KNOW this word.	I think I have heard this word.	I have NEVER seen this word.

2. Read through page 13. What is special about Nef's triangle?

   _____

3. Read through page 19. Look at the picture on page 18. Notice that one side of each square is also the length of the triangle's side.

4. What did Pythagoras notice when he added the tiles in the red and blue squares together?

   _____

   _____

5. Draw the red square, "a," the blue square, "b," and the largest square, "c." Label the length of the red square "a," the length of the blue square "b," and the length of the largest square "c." Label the right angle in the triangle.

   (Notice that the hypotenuse of the triangle is opposite of the right angle. This is always true in right triangles.)

6. Read through page 21. Express the area of each square using the variables you assigned to each length in Exercise 5.

   _____

(Continued)

LESSON PLAN 5-1 (Continued)

7. Read page 22. What relationship do you and Pythagoras notice about the squares built around a right triangle?

_____

_____

_____

_____

8. Read through page 24. In the box below, draw a picture representing a ladder 5 feet from a building that is 12 feet tall.

9. In your picture, label the hypotenuse, legs, and right angle of the triangle.

10. Now, use the pattern Pythagoras discovered to find out how tall the ladder needs to be to reach the top of the building. Show your work.

11. Read through page 29. Look at the map on page 29. Do you see the right triangle formed by the three islands? Which distance forms the hypotenuse of the triangle and which distances form the legs?

_____

_____

12. Use the pattern Pythagoras discovered to calculate the distance to Crete. Show your work.

13. Finish reading the book. In your own words, describe what the Pythagorean theorem is.

_____

_____

_____

14. Complete the following word problem: The legs of a right triangle are 6 feet and 8 feet long. What is the length of the hypotenuse? In the box below draw the triangle, and label the legs, hypotenuse, and right angle of the triangle.

> **Modifications for High School:** This activity focuses primarily on introducing the Pythagorean theorem, but is notable for proving it, which often does not come until later in mathematics. High school students can use the illustrations and basic proofs of the Pythagorean theorem to discuss trigonometric proofs of the theorem.

References

Anno, M. (1983). *Anno's mysterious multiplying jar* (M. Anno, Illus.). London: Bodley Head.

Campbell, S. C. (2010). *Growing patterns: Fibonacci numbers in nature* (S. Campbell & R. Campbell, Illus.). Honesdale, PA: Boyds Mill Press.

Common Core State Standards Initiative. (2010). *Common Core State Standards for English language arts & literacy in history/social studies, science, and technical subjects.* Washington, DC: National Governors Association Center for Best Practices and the Council of Chief State School Officers.

Ellis, J. (2004). *What's your angle, Pythagoras?* Watertown, MA: Charlesbridge Publishing.

Geisel, T. S. (1958). *The cat in the hat comes back.* New York: Random House Publishing.

Hennessy, B. G. (2004). *The once upon a time map book* (P. Joyce, Illus.). Somerville, MA: Candlewick Press.

McElligott, M. (2009). *The lion's share.* New York: Walker & Company.

Neuschwander, C. (1999). *Sir Cumference and the dragon of Pi* (W. Geehan, Illus.). Watertown, MA: Charlesbridge Publishing.

Neuschwander, C. (1999). *Sir Cumference and the first round table* (W. Geehan, Illus.). Watertown, MA: Charlesbridge Publishing.

Neuschwander, C. (2001). *Sir Cumference and the great knight of Angleland* (W. Geehan, Illus.). Watertown, MA: Charlesbridge Publishing.

Neuschwander, C. (2003). *Sir Cumference and the sword in the cone* (W. Geehan, Illus.). Watertown, MA: Charlesbridge Publishing.

Neuschwander, C. (2006). *Sir Cumference and the Isle of Immeter* (W. Geehan, Illus.). Watertown, MA: Charlesbridge Publishing.

Neuschwander, C. (2009). *Sir Cumference and all the king's tens* (W. Geehan, Illus.). Watertown, MA: Charlesbridge Publishing.

Schwartz, D. M. (1998). *G is for googol: A math alphabet book* (M. Moss, Illus.). San Francisco: Tricycle Press.

Schwartz, D. M. (1999). *On beyond a million: An amazing math journey* (P. Meisel, Illus.). New York: Random House.

Silvey, A. (2009). *Everything I need to know I learned from a children's book.* New York, NY: Roaring Brook Press.

Section III

Literacy and Mathematics in Culture

One of our primary motivations in writing this book is to remind readers that mathematics is everywhere. It is not limited to rules that must be memorized and problems that must be practiced. Mathematics is not something that can be contained in little boxes labeled "Arithmetic" and "Geometry" and "Calculus." Math describes the pinwheeling pattern of stars revolving overhead, and it guides the cartographer's hand in drawing the map that will bring a weary traveler home again.

We believe that students must be taught to recognize math when they meet it in their everyday worlds. This recognition will enhance their ability to grasp abstract concepts that are sometimes communicated best in arcane symbols like $<$ or $>$ or $+$ or $\int$ or ∞.

To this end, we have selected some examples of mathematics that can be found in far-flung corners of our culture like poetry, music, environmental print, social media, and computer gaming. The surprise experienced by a student who finds math in a computer game or a popular song will make a lifelong memory, and memories are at the root of all learning.

Throughout this section, we provide ideas for classroom activities and discussions. These are only the beginning. We hope that they provide models for you to use in designing your own activities to bridge the gap between math and the popular culture. Even more, we hope that they find their place in your students' minds, so that the day will come when they're listening to a complex beat pattern on the radio and they realize, "Hey, I just heard some math!"

We believe that offering students illustrations of applied mathematics from far-flung corners of the culture multiplies the chance that any given example will resonate with a particular student. Using a variety of reading strategies and activities is a useful strategy to help all students from all backgrounds become more cognizant of mathematics in their everyday lives.

Chapter 6

Poetry and Music: A Most Mathematical Approach to Words

POETRY

Poetry in the English language is no longer required to adhere to the prescribed rhythms of an earlier age. The advent of free verse—poetry without defined rhyme or rhythm schemes—freed poets from an unwavering devotion to rhyme and meter, but free verse is just one type of poem being written by modern poets. Poems do still rhyme sometimes, and sometimes, they do still follow a definable rhythm. At other times, poets play with their medium, twisting traditional forms such as sonnets and ballads into shapes that suit them. At still other times, poets leave familiar patterns behind completely and invent new ways to use language as an artistic medium.

Still, an artist needs to know the rules before breaking them. And the traditional rules of meter, in particular, have a mathematical flavor to them.

Math and Meter

For an artful introduction to the concept of meter and its relationship to language, introduce your students to the most famous purveyor of blank verse ever: William Shakespeare. We will refer to the following boxed passage, one of the most well-known poetic passages ever written in English, several times in this chapter. It will be used to define and illustrate "blank verse," so that we can use this form to illustrate several aspects of the mathematical basis of poetry.

In metered poetry, like the example passage, each line is divided into a regular number of accented and unaccented syllables: "That *thou* her *maid* art *far* more fair than *she*," for example, has four accented beats. The unaccented beats occur halfway between each accent. In the following line (written by this book's authors and *not* by Shakespeare), the unaccented syllables divide each beat into thirds: "In the *cool* of the *night*, crickets *sing* of the *time* when the *warm* wind will *blow*." And in the following author-generated line, the beats are divided into fourths: "After the *birth* of the gray *mead*owlark, I *sang*."

Reading these rhythmic lines aloud will give the study of fractions—halves, thirds, fourths—a visceral feel. Students can be given a standing assignment to listen to music, bringing in examples of songs where the beat is divided into halves, thirds, or fourths, with extra credit being given for unusual meters divided into five, six, or seven beats, or more.

In the following passage from *Romeo and Juliet*, is it a traditionally rhyming poem? Do any of the final words in these lines rhyme with any of the others?

Traditional rhyme requires both the ending consonants and the vowel sounds in the final syllable of two rhyming words to be the same, and the

---

But, soft, what light through yonder window breaks?
It is the east, and Juliet is the sun.
Arise, fair sun, and kill the envious moon,
Who is already sick and pale with grief
That thou her maid art far more fair than she.

(Shakespeare, c. 1590s, Romeo and Juliet, Act II, Scene II.)

line-ending words do not meet this criterion. (They could be said to have "slant rhyme," a poetic technique that relaxes some, but not all, of the familiar rules of rhymed poetry, but we will leave a formal definition of slant rhyme for another book. Our focus here is on poetic meter's function as a bridge between mathematics and language. Rhyme cannot be ignored, even in this sense, because it can serve to emphasize that meter, but it is not our focus in this text.)

Does the excerpt from *Romeo and Juliet* presented earlier display a regular meter, which is, along with rhyme, a key component of traditional poetry in the English language?

The first line is a sequence of alternating unstressed and stressed syllables that sound like this:

"da-DUHM da-DUHM da-DUHM da-DUHM da-DUHM"

The pattern "da-DUHM" is common in spoken English, so poets have given it a name: iamb. There are five iambs in this line, and this very common pattern is called "iambic pentameter." Unrhymed poetry written in iambic pentameter is called "blank verse," and much of Shakespeare's work is written in that meter.

"Pentameter," representing a poetic line that repeats the basic "foot" five times, is an example of a word with a Greek origin that students will see again in places outside the classroom. Of special interest to this discussion is the frequent appearance of words with the prefix "penta-" in mathematics. "Pentagon," a five-sided polygon, is one example. Other poetry-related words that demonstrate poetry's reliance on math, including prefixes used in naming polygons, are presented in the first activity at the end of this chapter, "Poetry Counts."

The concept of rhythm is closely related to the concept of time, and this link is yet another connection between a verbal art, poetry, and a quantitative concept that can be manipulated mathematically, time. English is known linguistically as a stress-timed language, meaning that, in general, English speakers adjust the timing of unstressed syllables so that the same amount of time passes between one stress and the next (Bertrán, 1999, pp. 103–104).

This speech pattern is called "stress-timing," and Bertrán called English the "stress-timed language *par excellence*" (p. 103). Bertrán quotes others who made much the same point, including Jones, who said, "There is a strong tendency in connected speech to make stressed syllables follow each other as nearly as possible at equal distances," Halliday, who said, "[...] there is a strong tendency in English for the salient syllables to occur at regular intervals; speakers of English like their feet to be all roughly the same length," and Bolinger, who said, "Speakers do adjust accents, where it is practical to do so (that is, where the stress and vowel structure permits), in order to GET roughly equal intervals" (Bertrán, 1999, pp. 103–130). In other words, the stressed syllables in English follow a regular beat, with the unstressed syllables between those stresses dividing those beats into equally divided parts—and once again, poetry has taken us back to the mathematical concept of fractions.

In contrast, many other languages are described as "syllable-timed," wherein the length of a spoken syllable is the unit that native speakers use to set the rhythm of their speech. Spanish is often given as a representative example of a syllable-timed language.

For a fun activity, have students read aloud the passage from *Romeo and Juliet* presented at the beginning of this section, and let them notice the spots where the meter varies slightly from iambic rhythm. "Juliet" might not have been the best name choice for a man working in iambic pentameter, since the two unaccented syllables at the end make it distinctly noniambic—unless Shakespeare pronounced her name as "JOOL-yet," as many British English speakers do, enabling him to tuck the name between an unaccented and an accented syllable. Similarly, "envious" might be pronounced as "EN-vyus," but "Who is already sick" seems to be missing an unaccented syllable from the beginning of the fourth line, and "already" isn't easily shoehorned into the iambic rhyme scheme.

Shakespeare took liberties with the meter because he was an artist and that's what artists do. But overall, this passage feels like iambic pentameter, and a very artful example, at that.

After students have explored the ways that Shakespeare followed strict iambic pentameter when it suited him and flouted it when it didn't, use the second classroom activity included at the end of this chapter, "Fractions, Poetic Meter, and Spoken English," to help them explore the rhythms of their own language.

MUSIC

Songs—music that is sung—are inextricably related to poetry. The need to fit lyrics to a rhythmic melody requires that they match the repetitive rhythm found in virtually all Western music. Take away the melody and musical instruments, and lyrics are nothing but rhythmic language—otherwise known as poetry. Therefore, the math-related observations we have made in the earlier poetry section are valid for lyrics, as well.

But what about the *music* part of a song—the melody and chord progressions? And what about instrumental music? Do they involve math, too?

This question reaches to the core of what music is—organized sound. And what is sound? Sound is caused by air vibrations that can be sensed by our ears.

Why do some of those vibrations sound different to us in a way that we describe as "higher" or "lower"? This is governed by the speed of those air vibrations. Now we are getting close to the mathematical heart of music, because the speed of the air vibrations can be expressed by a number, called the "frequency." The higher the frequency, the higher the note sounds to our ears. For example, the A above middle C on a piano has a frequency of 440 hertz (Hz). Any note that has a frequency greater than 440 Hz, be it 660 Hz or 880 Hz or whatever, will sound higher. (Or, rather, it will sound higher until the frequency gets so high that it can no longer be perceived by human ears.) Lower frequencies, such as 220 Hz, will produce lower tones as the frequencies decrease until they become so low that they are inaudible to the human ear.

Much of our perception of music is related to the distance between the tones. As a familiar example, the tones Do, Re, Mi, Fa, Sol, La, Ti, Do, which are known to anyone who has watched *The Sound of Music* (Chaplin & Wise, 1965) or heard the song *Do Re Mi*, describe a major scale. The frequency of the second Do in this scale, an octave above the first one, is twice the frequency of the first Do.

Thus, if we are looking at an A major scale beginning at A 440, the last note in the scale has a frequency of 880 Hz, for a ratio of 2.

The close relationship between musical pitch and the mathematical concept of ratios is explored in the third classroom activity at the end of this chapter entitled, "Relating Vibrational Frequency to Pitch with Ratios."

It is important to be aware that other cultures express music differently, and their scales and harmonies may sound very different from traditional Western music. The mathematics, however, still stands. The relationship between the frequencies of any two musical notes can be described in terms of a ratio. A great deal of research has been done in the area of music theory, studying these relationships between notes and the way they are perceived by human ears.

An interesting assignment for more advanced students wishing to explore further would be to ask them to research the music in one or more other cultures and compare it to our own familiar musical styles. What notes are used to construct scales in the musical systems of the cultures they have chosen?

A related assignment would be to ask students to research other tuning methods besides the "just intonation" method described earlier, such as well-tempered and equal-tempered tuning. How are they alike, and how are they different? Why might a musician choose one over another?

And, finally, an in-class discussion exploring all of the links between music and math that have been discussed here would not be complete without asking a simple question: Does this information change your appreciation of music? Do you enjoy knowing more about what you're hearing, or do you find that the knowledge distracts you from the art itself? Either answer is valid, but the discussion is an important one to have. The classroom activity entitled, "Rhythm and Language—Bringing Poetry, Music, and Mathematics Together" was designed to facilitate this discussion. It is included at the end of this chapter.

MATH AS A SPRINGBOARD TO VERBAL CREATIVITY

A relatively new poetic form called the "Fib" has been developed, using the Fibonacci sequence as a structure for creating poetry. Leonardo Fibonacci, a mathematician born in Italy in 1175, developed a series of numbers that was named after him, the Fibonacci sequence. This series begins with 0 and 1, and then continues infinitely, with each new number being the sum of the two previous numbers. The first thirteen numbers of the Fibonacci sequence are as follows:

0, 1, 1, 2, 3, 5, 8, 13, 21, 34, 55, 89, 144

A Fib generally uses the Fibonacci sequence to determine how many syllables are included on each line. Poems that are organized by the number of syllables per line are known as "syllabics" (Drury, 2006, p. 80). Because the line length increases quickly, most Fibs are relatively short poems with ten or fewer lines. The poet might also choose to let the Fibonacci sequence determine how many letters were in a line. Perhaps it would be a valid choice to begin someplace other than the start of the Fibonacci sequence, with a five-letter line, then an eight-letter line, and on and on. Or maybe the sequence could dictate the number of words per line. As in anything to do with poetry, the possibilities are endless (About Fibetry, 2010).

Have your students try writing Fibs, and let them experiment with all those options. Invite them to come up with their own options. Creativity in working with math *or* poetry is a valuable thing.

As an example, here is a Fib written by one of this book's authors:

Midsummer

A
splash
of red
on the smooth
green. Rosy freckles
signal ripeness. It will come, but
not tomorrow, nor tomorrow's tomorrow. Still, it
will come. At last, my teeth will break the tough red skin and the tomato's tart, melting flesh.

—Mary Anna Evans, 2010

Haiku is probably the best-known syllabic poetry form to English-speaking poets. Based on a Japanese form, English haiku are usually written in three lines, with the first and third lines having five syllables and the second line having seven syllables. A related form, the tanka, is slightly longer, with a five-seven-five-seven-seven syllable scheme (Drury, 2006, p. 81).

These two syllabic forms are frequently used in classroom settings, because their brevity makes it possible to write and discuss entire poems in a single class period. Yet there is much to learn from such deceptively simple rhythm schemes.

Perhaps there isn't a great deal of high-level mathematics to be learned from paring a poem down to seventeen or thirty-one syllables, but an innate feel for quantity can sometimes emerge in students who wrestle with numerical concepts in a way that hampers their progress into higher-level mathematics. This kind of counting—sensing syllables—is like the poetic rhythms discussed earlier, in that it can give a visceral sense of numbers to students who are kinesthetic learners, experiencing the world through their bodies.

Devoting 20 minutes of class time to writing a math-themed haiku or tanka after a grueling test can result in students who notice when a classmate cheats because a fifteen-syllable haiku just "feels" wrong. And from a literacy standpoint, the ability to clearly communicate a thought or feeling in just a few words is a life-enhancing skill to have.

To give your students an example of a math-themed syllabic poem, ask them to read the following tanka sequence by Johnny Masiulewicz, author of *Professional Cemetery* and *Keywords: A Dada Experiment*. Reading these sixty-two syllables would take less than a minute of class time but would provide a very approachable and human image for a calculus teacher who needed to illustrate the mathematical concept of the catenary—the shape in which an ideal chain (or, yes, a clothesline) will hang in the presence of gravity and the absence of other forces like wind or shirts.

the curvature of spacetime

however supreme-
ly taut the clothesline, it shall
curve inward to the
singularity, the point
where the mass of one shirt hangs
the quest for quantum
gravity goes on. and on.
the brainiacs are
using a loop theory bent.
puh-leeze. just look to the shirt

—Johnny Masiulewicz, 2010

Refer your students to Activity 5 at the end of this chapter for a reference to a website that offers an interactive demonstration comparing the shape of the catenary to the more familiar parabola.

For observations on a life spent on the boundary between poetry and mathematics, see the essay written by award-winning National Endowment for the Arts (NEA) Fellow Lola Haskins.

Loving Words the Way Zero Loves One

Lola Haskins

I wrote and published seven books of poems during the 28 years I taught programming at the University of Florida. And almost every time I'd give a poetry reading, someone in the audience would ask me how I could do two such different things. They aren't as different as people think, I'd explain, because doing either one well requires using both sides of your brain. When you write a program, you begin on the left, but if the problem is difficult, you often have to resort to the right to figure it out. Once you come up with an idea, you go back to the left to prove it's the solution. With poetry, you get something on paper using your right, your monkey mind, and then you use your left, your logic mind, to clean it up. Once you've done that, you go back to the right to see if it wants to go on. Then to the left again, and so on, until you're where you wanted to go. In other words, the methodological difference between poetry and math isn't that they use different sides of the brain. It's that in math, you start and finish with the left and in poetry, you start and finish with the right.

When I got tired of explaining all this the way I just have, I wrote a poem instead. Here it is, as it appeared in *Desire Lines, New and Selected Poems* (2004).

How do you reconcile teaching Computer Science with being a poet?

Either way, my hands move across the keys
even in the dark.
Either way, my fingers are not themselves,
tapping those little drums.

It is easy to love words the way zero loves one,
easy to take the sound that parts

(Continued)

the middle of the night
the way a boat's prow parts the sea—

was it an owl
was it a mouse, feeling something sharp lift its fur
and then it's flying

—and multiply it:
a blurred ring round the moon
the tossed rock of a man's heart,
as a woman lifts her bare arm.

A program calls across the gulf, just at dusk,
when the sun is the rose of a bird's egg,
and the subprogram replies.
She does not say what he thought she would.
He thought he knew her.
But no.

And you're sailing without your loran, which is blinking
incessantly, like someone startled by light
or someone trying all constellations at once.
And you surge hard against the black water,
dragging a trail of stars.
Steer now. Steer safe. Steer for the cooling towers
that rise like a city across the swells.

POETRY FOR POETRY'S SAKE

Lest we dissect the delicate art of poetry so completely that it loses its soul, it seems appropriate to close with a poem that acknowledges the hard-won knowledge of science and math, and then reminds us that, in life, there is so much more.

When I heard the learn'd astronomer
When the proofs, the figures were ranged in columns before me;
When I was shown the charts and the diagrams, to add, divide, and measure them;
When I, sitting, heard the astronomer, where he lectured with much applause in the lecture-room,
How soon, unaccountable, I became tired and sick;
Till rising and gliding out, I wander'd off by myself,
In the mystical moist night-air, and from time to time,
Look'd up in perfect silence at the stars.

—Walt Whitman, 1867

ACTIVITY 1: POETRY COUNTS

Poets describe the number of rhythmic feet in a poem's line with the following words, all of which use Greek prefixes to establish quantity (Drury, 2006, p. 65).

Monometer, one foot
Dimeter, two feet
Trimeter, three feet
Tetrameter, four feet
Pentameter, five feet
Hexameter, six feet
Heptameter, seven feet
Octameter, eight feet

An obvious mathematical connection to these poetic terms is the nomenclature of polygons, a closed plane figure bounded by straight lines (Merriam-Webster, 2010). While there cannot be a closed plane figure bounded by one or two straight lines, most of the other poetic prefixes have counterparts in the family of polygon names: triangle, pentagon, hexagon, heptagon, and octagon. The naming of polygons is included in the Common Core standards in grades 6 and 7 for geometry that require that students build on their work with shapes to determine area and work with polygons in the coordinate plane.

These poetic terms are linked to many other words that are used to specify quantity. Monofilament fishing line has but one strand. The octane rating of gasoline compares its combustion capability to pure octane, a hydrocarbon based on a chain of eight carbon atoms. A tetrahedron is a solid figure with four sides. Chemical nomenclature is inextricably linked to prefixes such as these that can quickly communicate important information on a molecule's structure (Merriam-Webster, 2010).

To explore the idea that quantity can be rapidly communicated by using words with these numerically based prefixes, assign students to collect such words. First, invite them to make a list of words they already know that are based on the Greek prefixes of the eight words above: mono-, di-, tri-, tetra-, penta-, hexa-, hepta-, and octa-. Then ask them, over a period of days or weeks, to keep notes on similar words that they hear in conversation or see in print. These notes should include the context of the encounter. This will enhance class interaction at the end of the assignment, when students can be encouraged to share where they heard or saw these words and asked whether they were familiar. Did knowledge of the prefix aid in decoding an unfamiliar word or a familiar word used in an unfamiliar way (Numerical Prefixes, 2008)?

ACTIVITY 2: FRACTIONS, POETIC METER, AND SPOKEN ENGLISH

Discuss with your class the concept of stress-timed and syllable-timed language, as presented in this chapter. Now, ask the students to notice their own speech patterns. Are their speech patterns stress-timed? Does the rhythm of their speech, whether they're singing, speaking, or reading poetry, remind them of fractions?

Play the students a recording of the famous "Blue Danube Waltz" by Johann Strauss. Can they hear that the beats are grouped into threes, with each beat representing a third of a measure? Now play them a recording of almost any rock or rap song. Can they hear that the beats are grouped into fours? Is it any wonder that a basic unit of music, the quarter note, has a name that is so obviously mathematically derived?

Now, ask for volunteers to read the earlier excerpt from *Romeo and Juliet* aloud, trying *not* to space the accents evenly. A metronome (which can be downloaded as a free smart phone app) can give audible guidance to students trying to space accents irregularly.

The volunteers will likely find this difficult, and their readings will sound awkward and jerky in a way that adolescents will probably find quite funny. You might suggest alternative speech patterns to the class—perhaps a reader could use syllables to mark the passage's rhythm. Is it comfortable to ignore stressed syllables, speaking three syllables for each tick of the metronome? Two? Five?

ACTIVITY 3: RELATING VIBRATIONAL FREQUENCY TO PITCH WITH RATIOS

As explained in the text, the frequencies of musical notes spaced one octave apart have a clearly defined ratio: Given the frequency of a note, the frequency of the note an octave above it is twice the frequency of the original note, a concept that is applicable to the Common Core Standards Ratios and Proportional Relationships for Grade 6 (Common Core State Standards Initiative, 2010).

To test your students' understanding of this concept of ratio in music, ask them this question: "If the E above middle C has a frequency of 660 Hz, name the frequencies of the next higher E and the next lower E?" (The answers are 1,320 Hz and 330 Hz.)

The frequencies of each of the other notes in the scale are defined by a ratio that relates them to the frequency of the root note, A 440. There are many different intonation systems to describe this sequence of ratios, but we have chosen a representation of "just intonation," which uses ratios that can be described by small integers, for simplicity's sake. The following table presents those ratios for each note in the A major scale.

The Mathematical Basis of the A Major Scale

Note	Interval	Ratio	Frequency
A	Root	1:1	440
B	Second	10:9	489
C#	Third	5:4	550
D	Fourth	4:3	587
E	Fifth	3:2	660
F#	Sixth	5:3	733
G#	Seventh	13:7	817
A	Eighth	2:1	880

We suggest that students who play instruments be invited to bring their instruments to class, as an aid to exploring this scale, as well as other examples in this section. In the absence of instruments, software is available to play musical notes on in-class computers. Electronic tuners often are capable of playing selected pitches, and apps are available to turn smart phones into electronic tuners. Physically produced musical notes, as opposed to electronic sounds, can be done easily and cheaply using a pitch pipe.

Now, as an exercise, use ratios to complete a similar table for a D major scale:

The Mathematical Basis for the E Major Scale

Note	Interval	Ratio	Frequency
E	Unison	1:1	660
F#	Second	10:9	___
G#	Third	5:4	___
A	Fourth	4:3	___
B	Fifth	3:2	___
C#	Sixth	5:3	___
D#	Seventh	13:7	___
E	Octave	2:1	___

Answers: F#: 733; G#: 825; A: 880; B: 990; C#: 1,100; D#: 1,226; E: 1,320

ACTIVITY 4: RHYTHM AND LANGUAGE—BRINGING POETRY, MUSIC, AND MATHEMATICS TOGETHER

Much of the popular music enjoyed all over the world has its origins in the New World, particularly rock and roll, jazz, blues, hip-hop, and rap. Music historians can trace the distinctive rhythms of these musical styles to Africa but, because they were developed in the United States, these musical forms were sung in English during their formative years.

Some questions for classroom discussion or written assignments might include these:

1. Did the use of English, a stress-timed language, affect the development of contemporary songs?
2. All forms of modern popular music are heavily influenced by rhythm. Rap, in particular, is highly dependent on the spacing of stressed syllables and on their interaction with a rhythm track, and this dependence is even more noticeable because the spoken-word flavor of rap isn't obscured by melody. Although there are African elements in those rhythms, the lyrics would interact far differently without the stress-timed patterns of spoken English. Would modern popular music as recorded in English, particularly rap, be a different art form if it had developed in a syllable-timed language such as Spanish?
3. Would rap, which generally consists entirely of the spoken word against a rhythmic background, sound the same when performed in a syllable-timed language? Would a person whose first language was not English hear those rhythms differently? Or might

a performance that sounds perfectly natural to an English speaker sound as alien and "wrong" as the exercise in this chapter instructing readers to read Shakespeare while ignoring the English speaker's instinct to place the language's stresses on rhythmic beats?

4. Prerecorded rhythm tracks can be downloaded to computers or smart phones for classroom listening. Invite students to compose their own brief raps, either individually or collaboratively. As volunteers perform them, ask the class to identify repeated rhythm patterns. Perhaps they will notice the iambs discussed in class. Then reverse the exercise. Ask students to compose a rap with a given rhyme scheme, such as iambic pentameter, and allow volunteers to demonstrate their interpretations. Students who are native speakers of non-English languages or who are studying a language foreign to them could be encouraged to complete this activity in a language other than English.

ACTIVITY 5: CATENARIES, LARGE AND SMALL—VISUAL CALCULUS

Catenaries are familiar shapes to those who look around them: Christmas lights draped across a house's eaves, clotheslines (for those students who have seen one in use), or the electrical cord of a smart phone charger dangling between phone and wall outlet. A string-like object that possesses weight will hang in a shape that approximates the ideal catenary if it is attached at both ends and allowed to hang free. A very large example of a catenary (or a real-life approximation thereof) stands in St. Louis as the famous Gateway Arch.

The mathematics of the catenary will be dealt with only in the most advanced high school calculus classes, but this doesn't preclude less advanced students from developing an intuitive feel for such shapes. Galileo himself believed that a hanging chain assumed the shape of a parabola. Close, but not quite . . .

The Wolfram Demonstrations Project's interactive website allows students to "play" with a hanging chain, and it shows them the catenary it forms, as well as the corresponding parabola, which doesn't *quite* fit the curve (Levart, 2011). It is a very hands-on example of the Common Core standards for High School Geometry: Modeling with Geometry, and Functions: Trigonometric Functions (Common Core State Standards Initiative, 2010). It is also applicable to the Grade 8 standard for geometry regarding understanding of congruence using physical models. See the demonstration page at http://demonstrations.wolfram.com/CatenaryTheHangingChain/.

Changing the virtual chain's length will show visually oriented students the difference between catenaries and parabolas, a concept we believe they will carry with them until they're ready for calculus—and perhaps the exploration itself will help make them ready for calculus.

References

About Fibetry. (2006, June). In *Fibetry.com*. Retrieved June 24, 2010, from http://www.fibetry.com/viewtopic.php?t=6/.

Bertrán, A. (1999). Prosodic typology: On the dichotomy between stress-timed and syllable-timed languages. *Language Design, 2*(2), 103–130.

Common Core State Standards Initiative. (2010). *Common Core State Standards for English language arts & literacy in history/social studies, science, and technical subjects.* Washington, DC: National Governors Association Center for Best Practices and the Council of Chief State School Officers.

Drury, J. (2006). *Creating poetry.* Cincinnati, OH: Writer's Digest Books.

Haskins, L. (2004). *Desire lines, new and selected poems.* Rochester, NY: BOA Editions.

Levart, B. (2011). *Catenary: The hanging chain.* Retrieved August 25, 2011, from http://demonstrations.wolfram.com/CatenaryTheHangingChain/.

Masiulewicz, J. "The Curvature of Space-Time". Unpublished manuscript.

Merriam-Webster. (2010). *Definition of "polygon."* Retrieved June 24, 2010, from http://www.merriam-webster.com/.

Numerical Prefixes. (2008). *Advanced English grammar.* Retrieved June 24, 2010, from http://advanced-english-grammar.com/numerical-prefixes.html/.

Shakespeare, W. (c. 1590s). *Romeo and Juliet.* From *The complete works of William Shakespeare* (World Library edition, 2000–2003). New York: HarperCollins.

Whitman, W. (1882). *Leaves of grass* (7th ed.). Boston: James R. Osgood and Company.

Wise, R. (Director/Producer). (1965). *The sound of music* [Motion picture]. United States: 20th Century Fox.

Chapter 7

Environmental Print: Math in Daily Life

INTRODUCTION

Ours is a literate society. A person who wanted to pass an entire day without seeing any written text would have to make a concerted effort. There could be no books or magazines in the house, unless they were stored on a bookshelf, pages pointing out. There could be no television viewing in that person's life. There could be no computer use and no Internet access. Contact with the outside world by mail would be impossible, although it would be possible to use the telephone, provided the phone had no screen displaying the number dialed or identifying the person who just called.

Even the simplest phone would likely have text on its plastic housing, requiring the careful literacy-phobe to ask someone literate to cover the brand name and serial number and the numbers on the buttons with duct tape—and that same task would have to be repeated on every household appliance. Packaged food would have to be removed from its packaging before entering this print-free household, although fresh fruit and vegetables in a plain bag would be safe.

Clothing would need to be searched carefully for tags that identified its manufacturer and gave instructions for laundering. As for actually *doing* the laundry, well, a washing machine and dryer would be very difficult to use without being able to choose the cycle or water temperature or drying time. And how would this be done if our imaginary literacy-phobe's assistant had already applied duct tape to those controls and removed the labels from the laundry detergent? It would be far safer to hand-wash the clothes in the kitchen sink with a bar of soap, except the soap would likely have its brand name stamped into the bar, and the faucet handles would almost certainly be labeled with an "H" and a "C."

Could our literacy-phobe ever leave the house? Not in a world with names printed on mailboxes and street signs on every corner and tremendous billboards trumpeting the virtues of commercial products for every eye to see.

There are still places in the world where someone who wanted to completely avoid the written word could hide, but they are widely scattered and increasingly rare. The written word has been ubiquitous in American culture almost since the country's inception; homes on the frontier might well have been print-free but, even there, packaged goods bought at a trading post often came in printed packaging. In cities, printed text would have been hard to avoid, even in 1776. Founding father Benjamin Franklin was a printer.

Yet further back in time, it *was* possible to live an entirely literacy-free life in the Western world. Certainly this was true before Gutenberg invented his printing press in 1450. Living in a society permeated with the printed word gives modern people a relationship with written language so engrained that it is hard to overstate its importance.

DEFINITION OF ENVIRONMENTAL PRINT

"Environmental print" is written language that is outside the traditional print media usually defined by books, newspapers, magazines, or formal written correspondence. It is not necessarily intended to be read from front to back for the purpose of following a defined storyline or logical argument. Environmental print can be an instruction manual or a piece of junk mail. It can be a sales pitch presented on a billboard or as part of a television commercial. It can be the instructions for playing the latest hot video game.

Much of the material on the Internet lives in a gray area between traditional print and environmental print. Traditional media, including well-known newspapers and magazines like *The New York Times* and *Newsweek* have online presences that are barely distinguishable from their print versions. Somehow, an unedited two-word Facebook status report written by a 12-year-old boy seems to belong in a different category. Perhaps environmental print is the best place to categorize it.

Still, one thing is indisputable. That two-word status report will be read by the 12-year-old's 739 Facebook friends. And if that 12-year-old tomorrow posts a hilarious story accompanied by a homemade video, he could find his video on YouTube going viral, and that bit of environmental print could find itself being read by 100,000 eyes.

In any book on literacy written in the twenty-first century, turning a blind eye to the explosion of user-generated environmental print and the corresponding explosion in the size of its readership would be unwise indeed.

Where to Find Environmental Print

Once your eyes have been opened to nontraditional sources of text, you will see opportunities everywhere for developing mathematical literacy. A trip to your mailbox will bring you junk mail that is chock-full of text explaining that you can have a brand new set of kitchen knives for a low payment of $29.99 (with fine print that states, "Plus 6 monthly payments of $29.99 and applicable state sales taxes").

Direct mail, websites, and television advertising are just a few sources of math lessons on fuzzy statistics. What does it really mean when an ad says that 97% of veterinarians agree that a particular liver-flavored toothpaste is an important contributor to your pet's dental health? Who conducted that study? How many veterinarians were consulted? How was the question posed to all those vets? Would their answer have been the same if the question had simply been, "Should owners brush their pet's teeth daily?" without specifying which brand of toothpaste should be used?

In looking for math in environmental print, it is often useful to "follow the money." Much environmental print is advertising copy, or it is funded by advertising. Thus, the numbers involved are often accompanied by dollar signs, and the profit motive is often accompanied by a motivation to use numbers to deceive. Such text offers yet another opportunity for a lack of literacy skills to result in financial losses. Combined with weak mathematical skills, that lack can prove devastating, leading to poor financial decisions made repeatedly over a lifetime. Teaching students to read persuasive pieces critically is an important life skill.

Teaching with environmental print offers the opportunity for homework assignments that are interesting and fun. Best of all, they cost nothing. A standing assignment to bring in examples of mathematics embedded in unexpected sources can generate animated class discussions on subjects that even you, the teacher, couldn't have anticipated—because you never know just what your students will find in their mailboxes.

IDEAS FOR USING ENVIRONMENTAL PRINT IN CLASS

In "Alternative Uses for Junk Mail: How Environmental Print Supports Math Literacy," Clark and Wallace (2007) describe a three-pronged plan that offers strategies for using environmental print in classroom projects of ever-increasing levels of complexity. In this section, we will present three suggested activities that are tied to each of these levels:

Level 1: Practicing Problems
Level 2: Constructing Knowledge About Problem Solving
Level 3: Thinking Critically About Mathematics and Literacy

A Level 1 Example: Checking the Fine Print for Ways to Practice Mathematical Skills

Retail sales have been revolutionized by the advent of the Internet. Shoppers never have to leave the comfort of their easy chairs, and they can comparison shop across websites worldwide. Students in their middle and high school years—students of the teachers who are the target audience for this book—are empowered by the ability to be consumers without the need for a car to get them to a store. The most significant constraint then becomes the necessity for access to a credit card or bank account for most purchases. Given access to a parent's credit card or bank account, a teen can, for good or ill, purchase nearly anything online.

The online shopping experience has some significant differences from shopping in a brick-and-mortar store. Those differences can affect prices, and they can add mathematical complexity to the not-trivial process of evaluating which item to purchase. Critical literacy skills are essential to detecting hidden costs or misleading offers. The ability to analyze text for bias requires an even more subtle interpretation of those offers. Are products offered on installment plans—"Only $99.99, or five monthly payments of $24.99 each!"—biased against consumers without the mathematical literacy to calculate the astronomical interest rate implicit in the installment offer?

Online purchases often require no sales tax, which decreases the out-of-pocket price significantly, but they do often require the purchaser to pay shipping and/or handling fees. These fees can vary by the size, weight, or cost of the object being purchased. Suddenly, a simple cost comparison can morph into an algebra problem.

For our example problem, let's consider an increasingly common situation, in which online retailers establish a loyalty club.

Members get free shipping, and sometimes they receive other perks like free express shipping. A prominent example is Amazon's "Amazon Prime" membership program. For our purposes, we'll use an imaginary program that is promoted with the following text. Some sample questions based on this text are included. We suggest completing this activity in class, then sending students home with an assignment to come back with similar advertisements for class discussion.

A Level 1 Activity: Find the Math in This Simulated Frequent Buyer Program

Ask the class for examples of frequent buyer programs, and ask them whether they or their parents are members of any such programs. Ask if they know what kinds of activities accrue benefits to the members and whether they know what those benefits are. Then present the following text to the class, asking them to read silently and be prepared to discuss its content, which includes concepts such as handling percent, decimals, and number operations included in the Common Core standards for Grades 6, 7, and 8 for Expressions and Equations, the Grade 8 standard for Functions, and the High School Functions standards for Interpreting Functions, Building Functions, and Linear, Quadratic, and Exponential Models. This example also addresses the High School Algebra Standards for Reasoning with Equations and Inequalities, Creating Equations, and Seeing Structure in Expressions (Common Core State Standards Initiative, 2010).

"Become a member of Math Insider and save! Buy all your school textbooks from our website and our low $5 per book shipping rate drops to zero. If your total textbook order exceeds $100, you'll also get a 10% discount on your entire order and a free protractor worth $3. Spend $200 and your discount increases to 20% on your entire order, and we'll throw in a calculator worth $15, along with that protractor! And how much do all the perks of being a Math Insider cost? Just $30. Order now!"

After the students have read the passage, ask for volunteers to explain the program to the class. Guide the discussion toward the following point: "Math Insiders" have three benefits—They have the opportunity to save on shipping, they can earn discounts, and they can earn free merchandise.

Ask students whether this seems like a mutually beneficial business relationship. Insiders can cut their costs, but they do have to spend money to do so. The textbook company makes less money, because of the cost of the free merchandise and shipping and because people are paying less for their books, but they presumably are making more sales.

Ask the class, "Under what circumstances could this relationship be detrimental to one party or the other?" Guide the students to the observation that consumers who don't need enough books to justify the $30 membership fee will lose money, even if they buy books they don't need to try to earn back their money. Conversely, the textbook company could see its profit margin shrink or disappear if the costs of free items and shipping aren't balanced by new sales.

Ask the class to work the following problems, and close the lesson by asking students to bring in frequent buyer offers that their family receives for future classroom discussion. Finally, guide the class in an exploration of their answers to the written questions. In particular, remind the students of the last question asked before the problems were worked: "Under what circumstances could this relationship be detrimental to one party or the other?" If their answers have changed after working the problems, facilitate a discussion of why those answers changed.

1. If textbooks are $40 each, how many must a Math Insider purchase to earn the free protractor? How much would the Insider save, compared to buying those textbooks without the discount and free shipping?

Answer: Without the Math Insider plan, those textbooks would have cost $120, plus $15 shipping, or $135. With the plan, the textbooks will cost $120, less 10%, or $108, for a savings of $27. If the purchaser actually needed the protractor and would have bought it anyway, then those savings increase to $30.

2. If a non-Insider wanted to buy three textbooks that have a regular price of $40 each, would it be worthwhile to join the Math Insider program?

    Answer: As shown in the answer to Question 1, buying three textbooks brings about a savings of $27, which is less than the cost to join the program. However, if the person needed a protractor and would have bought one anyway, the additional $3 savings brings the total savings to $30. In other words, this is the break-even point. If the purchaser did not need a protractor, he or she would need to purchase one more book to pass the break-even point. It is a toss-up as to whether purchasing a Math Insider membership is beneficial. However, if the purchaser is reasonably certain of the need to purchase more textbooks later, membership begins to look more like a good deal.

3. If an Insider purchases seven $40 books, what is the total out-of-pocket cost? What would be the total out-of-pocket cost for the same purchase if the purchaser is not a member of the Insider program? Express the Insider's cost as a percentage of the total nonmember cost.

    Answer: A non-Insider would pay 7 × $40, or $280, for the books, plus 7 × 5, or $35, for shipping. An Insider would pay no shipping. Because the bill is over $200, the Insider would qualify for a 20% discount of $56. The final bill is $280 – $56, or $224, and the Insider will also earn a free protractor and a free calculator, which have value if the buyer needed them and would have purchased them anyway. The final bill does not reflect the $30 cost of joining the Insider program, but the savings exceed $30, so this purchase alone will justify the cost of joining. The Insider's cost of $224 is 80% of $280.

4a. Write a discontinuous function to describe the cost per book as a function of the number of books purchased. Assume that the base cost, without discounts, of each book is $20. (Omit the free protractor and calculator and work only with the cost of the books and shipping.) Let N equal the number of books purchased, and C equal the cost per book in dollars.

    Answer:

    $$C = \begin{cases} 25N, \text{ if } N \le 5 & \text{(Full cost is \$20 plus \$5 shipping. No discount if fewer} \\ & \text{than 5 books bought, for a total of \$100.)} \\ 18N, \text{ if } 5 \le N \le 10 & \text{(First-level discount, 10\% of \$20, yields per-book} \\ & \text{cost of \$18. Shipping is now free.)} \\ 16N, \text{ if } N \ge 10 & \text{(Second-level discount, 20\% of \$20, yields per-book} \\ & \text{cost of \$16. Shipping is still free.)} \end{cases}$$

4b. Presume that our Insider did want the $3 protractor and the $15 calculator. Rewrite the discontinuous function from Question 4a to include the benefit the Insider is getting from the program. (Hint: Subtract the value of the free merchandise from the appropriate function[s].)

(Continued)

> **Answer:**
>
> $$C = \begin{cases} 25N, \text{ if } N \le 5 & \text{(Full cost is \$20 plus \$5 shipping. No discount if fewer than 5 books bought, for a total of \$100.)} \\ 18N - 3, \text{ if } 5 \le N \le 10 & \text{(First-level discount, 10\% of \$20, yields per book cost of \$18. Shipping is now free.)} \\ 16N - 28, \text{ if } N \ge 10 & \text{(Second-level discount, 20\% of \$20, yields per book cost of \$16. Shipping is still free.)} \end{cases}$$

A Level 2 Example: Assembling Knowledge as It Pertains to Citizenship—The Impact of Polls on Elections

Political polls are reported in virtually every newspaper, on virtually every broadcast news show, and on virtually every news-oriented website, and those reports appear almost every day. They appear in advertisements, and they arrive in our mailboxes in the form of campaign materials, which are particularly tricky to interpret, when the fact that they were produced by advertising agencies with political agendas is taken into account. When you are told that a poll has revealed that one candidate is favored by 62% of voters, can you really take the information seriously?

Gallup is an organization that has provided polling services and consultation for more than 75 years. It is a familiar name to anyone who follows news and politics, and its website (www.gallup.com) is a useful tool to teachers who wish to use polling as a mathematical teaching tool.

On the daily news page, Gallup offers a simple graphic tracking important ratings, including, at the time of this writing, an economic confidence index, underemployment statistics, a job creation index, a consumer spending index, and a presidential approval rating. Brief news articles on this page highlight current events that are believed to be affecting these indices, as well as other information gained by polling that is of interest to the general public. These articles might present the results of a poll that found patriotism to be on the rise, or they might report on the apparent effects of an incident like the Deepwater Horizon oil spill on the president's popularity or on consumer spending.

Of particular interest on the Gallup site is a page that briefly explains the organization's polling methodology, with a link to more in-depth information at Gallup's page titled, "How Does Gallup Polling Work?" (Gallup, n.d.). It describes Gallup's approach to contacting Americans over 18 by landline and cell phone, and it clarifies issues such as whether unlisted phone numbers are included in the sampling. A brief summary of the statistical basis of these methods is included.

To prepare for classroom discussion, ask students to read this article, and then use the following open-ended questions to prompt classroom discussion.

As homework, students could be directed to investigate other polling organizations by reviewing the organizations' websites and reporting on differences between polling methods and results. Do any of the organizations appear to have biases detectable on their websites? Do any of them report significantly different results from other polling organizations on major indices like consumer confidence or presidential approval? If so, are the sources of that variation apparent from an

A Level 2 Activity: A Poll Is Only as Good as the Questions Asked

After students read the Gallup article silently, ask them whether they have questions regarding the vocabulary of the article and whether they felt that they were able to grasp its intent. Interpretation of such data draws from sophisticated skill sets that include the ability to glean information from information presented in table form, as well as a strong enough grasp of statistics to be able to evaluate whether a given study was well constructed. These skills are included in all of Common Core's Statistics and Probability Standards, from grade 6 through high school (Common Core State Standards Initiative, 2010). After clarifying any issues regarding the article's meaning, use the following questions to facilitate discussion of polling methods, based on what the students gleaned from the article.

1. Does Gallup's methodology seem sound? Polling is done by landline telephones and by cell phones, which is an extension of the long-used method of polling by landline. Do you think results would differ if no effort were made to reach individuals by cell phone? Would the population polled differ in age? Political opinion? Income level? Level of education? Do you think it is significant that polling by phone excludes many or most homeless people? What about transient populations, such as migrant workers? Is there any way to know whether a significant portion of these populations have cell phones, or whether their opinions are included in polls?

2. Do you think it would be worthwhile for Gallup to extend polling to include electronic communication like email and social media? Should they go *back* in time, communication-wise, and do some polling face-to-face to capture individuals without access to a telephone and electronic communication?

3. Randomly asking political questions of anyone who owns a phone does not take into account voting behavior or even voting eligibility. Are there changes in polling methods that might capture a higher or lower percentage of children or adults who are not registered to vote?

4. How might the choice of wording of a poll's questions affect results? Do you think the response might be different in a poll of presidential performance if subtle wording changes communicated varying levels of respect? For example, might there be a difference in response between the following three questions: "What do you think of President Jane Smith's performance?" "What do you think of Jane Smith's performance as president?" "Do you approve of Smith as a president?"

examination of polling methods or possible political biases? Or can they be explained by the expected range of uncertainty of the research methods being used?

A Level 3 Example: Think Critically About Research Studies—Do Statistics Lie?

The Chronicle of Higher Education recently reported on two conflicting studies on social media usage. The report, "Facebooking Won't Affect Your Grades, Study Finds. At Least Until Next Month's Study Tells You It Will," is a very brief overview that gives links to more in-depth information on the studies in question (Parry, 2010).

One study, conducted at the University of New Hampshire, showed no statistical correlation between grades and usage of social media such as Facebook.

The other study, conducted at Ohio State University, showed that nonusers of Facebook earned higher grades than students who used Facebook.

Do these two studies contradict each other? Perhaps. But a careful reading of *The Chronicle of Higher Education* article reveals a need for caution in drawing conclusions, even though these studies both originated at major universities and were reported on the websites of reputable journals.

A Level 3 Activity: Thinking Critically—How Can Two Contradictory Studies Both Be True?

In preparation for this activity, have your students access the web page address for the Parry (2010) study in this chapter's bibliography, and ask them to read the brief article posted there. Then use the points below to facilitate class discussion.

Like the previous activity, interpreting the material presented in this article requires a sophisticated grasp of statistics, as well as the analytical skills to be able to evaluate whether a given study was well constructed. Some of the skills required are included in all of Common Core's Statistics and Probability Standards, from Grade 6 through high school (Common Core State Standards Initiative, 2010).

First, ask students to consider the source of their information. The *Chronicle* article was first published as part of a blog. It appears to report the two scholarly publications, summarizing results complete with numbers and percentages, but it is not itself a scholarly, peer-reviewed publication. And it is not presented as such. The title is humorous, and the article itself offers a light-hearted look at the changing state of science, in which succeeding studies contradict each other with regularity.

To the author's credit, he gives links to his original sources. As a second spur for class discussion, ask your students to read the material he references in order to prepare for a more in-depth class discussion. Some questions you might ask to provoke classroom discussion include the following.

1. Are these studies truly contradictory? One study says that social media like Facebook, Twitter, and other sites were found to have no effect on college students' grades. The other study focused on Facebook only and found that it *did* affect grades. Can you determine from a reading of the materials presented whether it is possible that Facebook depresses grades, but other social media do not, or that they may even be related to higher grades?
2. Both studies focused on college students. Do you think the results can be extrapolated to high school students? Why or why not?
3. The sizes of the two studies were radically different. The University of New Hampshire researchers studied 1,127 students, whereas the Ohio State University group looked at 102 undergraduate and 117 graduate students. Without a thorough understanding of the statistical concepts involved in designing a research study, do you feel comfortable saying that the smaller study does as good a job of predicting reality as the larger one? And are undergraduate students really comparable to graduate students in their study behavior? If not, then the smaller study's sample size drops from 219 individuals to 102. Can you say whether either sample size was large enough to be statistically significant?
4. How would you design a similar study for your school? What questions would you ask students? Would you limit your investigation to Facebook, or would you include other social media? How would you measure a student's social media usage? And how would you assess that student's academic performance?

SO WHAT? USING MATH TO MAKE PEOPLE CARE

Numbers occupy a peculiar place in the human psyche. They give the impression of specificity and reality. A marketing piece that claims, "Almost everybody loves our chewing gum!" has nowhere near the power of a piece that trumpets, "Nine out of ten chewers prefer our gum!" Because of this power, environmental print is infused with mathematical references that can be used in the classroom to reinforce abstract concepts. As a by-product, students learn an important life skill; they learn to consider the source of the information they use in their daily lives.

This higher-level thinking is a key by-product of studying mathematics, and it is one of the reasons our educational system requires students to learn math at a level far beyond that needed to balance a checkbook. Devoting class time to a careful review of the text bombarding modern humans in the form of environmental text is an excellent way to marry the theoretical aspects of mathematics with its practical applications.

References

Clark, K. K., & Wallace, F. H. (2007). Alternative uses for junk mail: How environmental print supports mathematical literacy. *Mathematics Teaching in the Middle School, 12*(6), 326–332.

Common Core State Standards Initiative. (2010). *Common Core State Standards for English language arts & literacy in history/social studies, science, and technical subjects.* Washington, DC: National Governors Association Center for Best Practices and the Council of Chief State School Officers.

Gallup. (n.d.). *How does Gallup polling work?* Retrieved July 5, 2010, from http://www.gallup.com/poll/101872/How-does-Gallup-polling-work.aspx.

Parry, M. (2010). Facebooking won't affect your grades, study finds. At least until next month's study tells you it will. *The Chronicle of Higher Education.* Retrieved July 5, 2010, from http://chronicle.com/blogPost/Facebooking-Wont-Affect-Your/19551.

Chapter 8

Math Literacy and
the Electronic Culture:
Social Media, Gaming,
and Reality Shows

INTRODUCTION

The World-Wide Web has radically increased the value of written communication. Notice that even its name, World-Wide Web, signifies a new form of communication that spans the globe. The desire to communicate with a child in Australia who enjoys the same video games as they do has compelled many young people who would never voluntarily write a paper on the subject to compose many, many pages of emails, texts, and tweets.

But what are we, as educators and authors, to do within an environment that is in constant flux? Facebook and Twitter dominate the electronic world as we write this book. Even if there were no lag time between our writing and your reading, the electronic world moves on, and something else may have supplanted those two juggernauts for the attention of your students by the time you're ready to use concepts you've learned here in your classroom. In a mutable world, how do we give you the information you will need for your students tomorrow, next week, or next year?

Put simply, we decided to go with what works. People are eternally fascinated with each other; Facebook and Twitter are only the most recent social tools in our arsenal. When something new supplants them, it's a good bet that the activity we've developed for today's electronic tools will still work with Twitter's replacement, whatever it is. Archaeologists tell us that people have played games from time immemorial. If our featured game, *FarmVille*, drops off the electronic map, we feel sure that more games will arise that will use math in much the same way. And if we look at this chapter's discussion of *American Idol* as an investigation of the electoral process, we will see that there will always be a way for residents of nations with an electoral tradition to make themselves heard—and those ways will always involve math.

SOCIAL MEDIA

Social media, with the networking site Facebook currently in the lead, are transforming an activity as old and as human as making friends, except "making friends" is a quaint phrase that has been replaced by the new verb "friend." The English language adapted to this new world yet again in 2009, when "unfriend" was named the word of the year by the New Oxford American dictionary (Gross, 2010). With 2011 arrived the inclusion of the word "tweet" into Merriam-Webster's dictionary (O'Toole, 2011).

Any casual observation of middle and high school students in their free time will reveal the obvious: Their social interaction is largely conducted through text messages, tweets, social networking, instant messages, and, although it is increasingly passé, email. Parents report that cell phone usage has shifted strongly away from actually talking on the phone toward text messaging, and this is being confirmed by formal polling agencies (Murphy, 2010).

At the end of this chapter, you'll find Activity 1, which takes advantage of the World-Wide Web's interconnectedness.

A WORD ABOUT CONSTANT CHANGE: HOW WILL YOU DEAL WITH IT OVER THE COURSE OF YOUR CAREER?

Students are reading, writing, and just generally working with text in their spare time, and they're doing a lot of it. While the literary value of "Zup?" and "Kewl!" (also known as "What's up?" and "Cool!" for the uninitiated) can be debated, there's no question that a great deal of written communication is taking place.

At this point in the discussion, we'd like to pause and talk about the rate of change in technology that our society is experiencing. The authors of this book represent a reasonably wide age range—at the time of this writing, Faith is in her thirties and Mary Anna is in her forties, and our contributor, Megan, is in her twenties—but the age range of this book's readership is wider still, and this gradient is not insignificant when we are writing about technology. As we write, we envision this book in the hands of preservice teachers, many of whom are in their early twenties, as well as graduate students, university professors, and in-service teachers who may be of any age.

While all three of us would be able to decode "Zup?" if it appeared as a text message, through interaction with our children, our students, or our peers, it is entirely reasonable to assume that an in-service teacher with 40 years of classroom experience might not. Thus, we have given considerable thought to the best way to present material in this chapter. We have elected to focus on the parts of the technological experience that do not change. Computer games, like low-tech board games, engage players with challenging play and with appealing back stories. Social media fascinates us because we are social creatures, and the World-Wide Web has given us the opportunity to reach out to everybody. Interactive reality shows touch the same part of our psyche as democratic government; everyone wants to feel that they have a voice.

For those of you who feel intimidated by this brave new world, our eldest author would like you to know that she earned a master's degree in chemical engineering in 1984 by writing a computer program in FORTRAN that solved a system of partial differential equations that described the chemical kinetics of ammonia, oxygen, and nitrous oxide. It took a mainframe computer 2 hours to churn through the calculations each time she changed the parameters and ran it again. Nowadays, FORTRAN is a dead language, and Mary Anna is pretty sure that her mammoth program, with all its variations in parameters, would now run in an instant on the phone in her hip pocket.

Does she feel obsolete, despite the fact that she expects another 15 or 20 years of work life before she retires? Oh, heck no. She feels that the problem-solving and analytical skills she developed in 1984 will stand her in good stead as the winds of technological change continue to howl.

If you are an in-service teacher who is feeling intimidated by the thought of putting new technology to work in your classroom, set the uncertainty aside and dive in. Your students would probably enjoy helping you, and the analytical skills you earned through the study of mathematics will carry you through. If you're a 22-year-old recent graduate who's feeling pretty cocky about such things, hang on. Things will change, but you'll be ready.

GAMES AND THEIR RELATIONSHIP TO MATH AND LITERACY

Any encounter with a computer has a mathematics-related tinge, even in today's world of increasingly user-friendly and intuitive interfaces. The human–computer relationship still requires an organic being with an intuitive and not-always-logical brain to communicate with a machine that thinks according to fixed rules. And it does that while thinking in terms of 1s and 0s.

Logic is mathematics' twin sister, and if you listen to students talk as they interact with a balky computer, you will hear logic in action.

"Why won't it recognize my password?"

"Did you check the caps lock key? I think that site is case-sensitive."

"This new program won't load."

"Maybe you've got a window open somewhere. Let me check . . ."

If your finger slips and you type www.microsoft.cim, any human being would know that you meant www.microsoft.com, but, last time we checked, Internet Explorer—Microsoft's *very own web browser* told us that this URL was not valid. A human being would have just sent us on to the actual website with an eye-rolling sigh.

Computers are force-feeding an entire generation with the fundamentals of logic. Actually, they've been doing that for a least a generation, maybe two, but today's students were born into houses with computers, and the cohort that was born into homes that were connected to the Internet is now arriving in America's high schools, even as this book is being written. If only there was a way to use this wave of change to foster literacy and mathematical competency.

But perhaps there is. Video and computer gaming has been with us for decades, but the social networking world is transforming games as well. Gamers interact through their gaming consoles or through sites like Facebook that offer them the opportunity to play with people all over the world. They can compete. They can collaborate. And some of the most popular games are based on math.

So let's let kids play games at school. It's not a new idea. Besides, there's a whole branch of mathematics called game theory. If the big guys do it, why shouldn't our young students? But which games should we use?

A very popular type of game allows players to simulate real-world situations, and those simulations are rooted heavily in mathematical concepts, particularly modeling. While playing these games, gamers can run a restaurant, design an amusement park, or operate a lemonade stand. If an imaginary world can be animated, then a game can be designed for it. We would like to investigate the opportunities for learning math through gaming.

(Here, we encounter an important difficulty in writing about mathematics in popular culture. That culture can change a great deal in the year that a book is in production and the years that a book is in print. Today's hot computer game becomes . . . well . . . yesterday's hot computer game. Yet educators cannot afford to ignore a phenomenon that is so powerful in today's youth culture. Our hope is that if the games mentioned here should ever become unavailable, there is enough information here to help teachers find other games with similar educational possibilities.)

Simulation Games: The Algebra Connection

A number of popular games allow the player to design a business, character(s), or situation, and then watch as the computer predicts how successfully this scenario operates in the real world. Enduring examples of such games include Hasbro Interactive's *RollerCoaster Tycoon* (originally published 1999 and, at the time of this writing, preparing for the rollout of its fourth edition), in which players design, build, and operate a theme park, and Electronic Arts' *The Sims* (Maxis, 2000) (originally published in 2000, with expansion packs to 2009's third edition still being released at the time of this writing), in which the player creates and guides a family through a simulated life. The underpinnings of the computer programs running these games are often based on algebra, and the overarching goal of game play is to model a real-world scenario in a way that the game predicts will be successful.

One such game that is popular at the time of this writing, *FarmVille* (Zynga, 2009), allows players to earn money, known as *FarmVille* coins, by planting crops. We have chosen to feature *FarmVille* for some specific reasons. It is a well-developed example of a simulation game. Its recent popularity increases the likelihood that it will remain available, even when it is supplanted by the next hot game. It does not require gamers to shoot people or to otherwise commit violence. (One presumes that livestock, once sold, is killed and eaten, but students who object can choose not to sell livestock, taking this into account when they develop their farms.) The ability to design one's own farm is an exercise in creativity. *FarmVille* is free. It is available on Facebook, allowing interaction and collaboration worldwide. Finally, this book's authors think that *FarmVille* is fun.

As students play the game, they learn that plowing and planting a *FarmVille* field cost coins, just as they do in real life, as do buying trees and livestock. Different crops ripen at different rates, and they can be sold for differing amounts. Equipment to grow these crops and structures in which to store them are available, but they cost coins, and the player must decide whether purchasing them will be cost effective for the farm.

In other words, the profitability of any crop can be described with math, specifically through linear equations, and simulating the farm's profitability through the simultaneous solution of all those linear equations is a working example of mathematical modeling, which is addressed in the high school Common Core standards. Standards addressed during our exploration of *FarmVille* include Grades 6, 7, and 8, Expressions and Equations, Grade 8 Functions, and the High School Algebra categories of Seeing Structure in Expressions, Creating Equations, and Reasoning with Equations and Inequalities, as well as the High School Functions categories of Interpreting Functions, Building Functions, and Linear, Quadratic, and Trigonometric Functions (Common Core State Standards Initiative, 2010).

Let's look at the algebraic equations that *FarmVille* players handle every time they play the game, without even thinking about it.

Arithmetic

A field of strawberries costs 15 coins to plow and 10 coins for seeds to plant the berries. The field can be harvested in 4 hours, yielding 35 coins.

Blueberries also ripen in 4 hours, and they also cost 15 coins for plowing. At 50 coins, the seeds are much more expensive to plant, but harvest yields 91 coins.

Simple arithmetic tells us that strawberries will yield 10 coins of profit in 4 hours.

> Strawberry sale price − Total cost to plant = profit
> 35 − (15 + 10) = 10

Blueberries, however, will yield 26 coins.

> Blueberry sale price − Total cost to plant = profit
> 91 − (15 + 50) = 26

By playing the game, students will quickly develop their own strategies for determining which crops to plant. In this instance, blueberries are clearly more profitable, but might not be the best choice for a farmer whose funds for buying seeds are limited. Farmers on tight budgets can still profit from strawberries, but their profits will accrue more slowly.

Ratios and Rates

It was easy to compare the profitability of strawberries and blueberries, because they ripened at the same rate—once every 4 hours. Ratios are a useful way to compare crops that ripen at different rates. Crops can be assessed on an equal basis by looking at their profitability in coins per hour.

Consider strawberries, pumpkins, rice, and cranberries:

> *FarmVille* strawberries ripen in 4 hours, seeds are 10 coins, and plowing is 15 coins. They sell for 35 coins.
> (35 − 10 − 15) coins/4 hours = 2.5 coins/hour
>
> Pumpkins ripen in 8 hours, seeds are 30 coins, and plowing is 15 coins. They sell for 68 coins.
> (68 − 30 − 15) coins/8 hours = 2.875 coins/hour
>
> Rice ripens in 12 hours, seeds are 45 coins, and plowing is 15 coins. It sells for 96 coins.
> (96 − 45 − 15) coins/12 hours = 3 coins/hour
>
> Cranberries ripen in 10 hours, seeds are 55 coins, and plowing is 15 coins. They sell for 98 coins.
> (98 − 55 − 15) coins/10 hours = 2.8 coins/hour

Clearly, if you have enough money to purchase rice, and you can wait 12 hours to receive your income, rice is the most cost-effective crop to grow. But if you need the money in 4 hours, then you must be satisfied with a less profitable crop, strawberries. Conversely, if you don't want to be chained to your computer, harvesting strawberries every four hours around the clock, then rice might be a more effective use of your time. (And, teachers, math class is as good a place as any to encourage students to take a clear look at the amount of time they spend gaming and socializing online.)

Linear Equations

Students who have had hands-on experience watching their computer-generated crops ripen at different rates, yielding differing amounts of profit, will have seen linear equations in action. This is quite a different experience from simply plotting x-y charts in a classroom.

The rates calculated earlier can be used to write linear equations for the profit on each different crop, in terms of coins (C) and hours (H):

Strawberries:
$$C = 2.5H$$

Pumpkins:
$$C = 2.875H$$

Rice:
$$C = 3H$$

Cranberries:
$$C = 2.8H$$

Plotting these equations is a useful exercise that will help students grasp the real-world applications of the concept of slope. *FarmVille* players quickly grasp that the slope of these graphs shows them just how fast their coins will pile up!

Other Opportunities to Enhance Literacy Using Computer Gaming

There are active online communities where players discuss game details and strategies. The companies producing the games often maintain websites and mailing lists to alert players to new features and upcoming improvements. Enthusiastic gamers can learn about "Easter eggs" hidden in the game code, which provide unexpected rewards for seemingly random activities. All of these communities and websites require reading and interpreting text that often has significant mathematical content.

Some websites go beyond describing winning strategies and Easter eggs, entering the realm of "cheats," which exploit weaknesses in programming to enable the player to score higher or acquire items that will help them in the game or that are just plain fun. Some of these cheats have a mathematical basis—for example, *FarmVille* players can position hay bales in a particular configuration that will prevent their farmer from taking up time walking across their farm. This cheat could trigger classroom conversation on the potential distance that the farmer might ordinarily walk and on the value of the time this cheat will save. In addition, the very existence of cheats can steer classroom conversation to the math-related topic of logic and the not-so-math-related but important topic of ethics.

Gaming stopped being done at a kitchen table with a board game on a Saturday night at about the time *Pong* and *Pac-Man* blipped onto our cultural scene. Now, game apps are available for even the smallest handheld phones, and they can be downloaded instantly almost anywhere.

(Let's pause for a moment to consider why it's necessary for a high-level player to look to Malaysia or Bolivia or Egypt for worthy competitors. It probably says something essential about our nature that, although the computer in our lap might be an excellent computer that could deliver a highly challenging round of whatever game you like to play, people seek out other people for play. Although they are not strictly mathematical questions, it might be worth a few minutes of class time to ask the following questions: Why do you play games? Would you prefer to play the computer or an opponent in another country whom you will never meet? What is the difference between the two?)

Geometry in Computer Gaming

The location of every pixel on a computer screen can be described as a point on a Cartesian plane, and this is often critical to the design of computer games. Once a student is made aware of this design element, the fact that the playing field is a Cartesian plane is almost always evident to the player.

When a player designs a city while playing the latest version of *SimCity*, with iterations currently including *SimCity 4* and *SimCity Societies* (Maxis & Nintendo EAD, 1989), or a theme park using *RollerCoaster Tycoon*, with its fourth edition due out as this book is being written (MicroProse, 1999), the playing area is divided into a grid. To build a skyscraper or a roller coaster, the player must tell the computer where to put it on that grid, and this is an obvious example of a Cartesian plane at work. Cartesian coordinate systems are addressed at all levels of the Common Core systems of standards. Familiarity with describing shapes on a number line or a two- or three-dimensional grid is essential to grasping many mathematical concepts. How interesting it is that, for a logical system like a computer, x-y coordinates are an even more essential way to navigate. Think about how humans give directions.

Go through two stop signs then look to your left just as the road turns right. Well, not when it goes a little to the right. Wait till it makes a real hairpin, then look left and you'll see the sign for our neighborhood. Go into the neighborhood and take the first left after the dark gray house with the basketball goal in the driveway . . .

Such directions would give a computer (or its programmer) real heartburn. But tell that computer to pinpoint a location thirteen units left and twelve units below a predetermined origin point, and it will be able to highlight that spot for you in an instant.

Worthwhile classroom conversation can be had about the ultimate reason x-y coordinate systems are everywhere: They are a very easy way to let other people know how to find a particular spot.

TELEVISION REALITY SHOWS

"Reality shows" are a relatively recent genre of television programming. They vary widely in theme, but they have a few things in common. They feature people who are not actors or are purportedly not acting in the context of the show. They are said to be unscripted and to document actual events.

These concepts have been applied to a wide variety of programming. There have been documentary-like shows, such as *The Real World* (Bunim & Murray, 1992) or *The Osbournes* (Taylor, 2002), that take cameras into the day-to-day personal lives of ordinary people and celebrities. *COPS* (Langley & Barbour, 1989) was the first hit show of many that have taken viewers into the professional lives of people with interesting or dangerous jobs. Makeover shows like *The Biggest Loser* (Broome, 2004) and *What Not to Wear* (BBC Productions USA, 2003) depict people being advised by experts on self-improvement activities like weight loss and image. Shows like *Extreme Makeover: Home Edition* (Endemol, 2003) and *While You Were Out* (Halaban, 2002) do the same for participants' homes. Hidden camera series like *Punk'd* (Kutcher & Goldberg, 2003) hark back to the days when *Candid Camera* (Funt, 1948) recorded the reactions of unsuspecting people to over-the-top hoaxes. But the most interesting category for the purposes of this book includes the shows whose outcome depends on the voting behavior of at-home viewers, like *American Idol* (Fuller, 2002) and *Dancing with the Stars* (BBC Worldwide, 2005).

American Idol is currently the most prominent example of this genre of reality show. While television scheduling can be expected to change during the period while this book is being published and is in print, *American Idol* is currently under contract through 2013, and it is an excellent example of the audience participation format. We have chosen to highlight the mathematics inherent in this format by giving *American Idol* as an example, with the understanding that the principles carry through to other similar shows.

So let's look at the workings of this juggernaut—the top-rated show for 8 years running (Answers.com, 2010). How does America vote for its idol? How are those votes counted? Is the result representative of the country at large? And how can you use this information in your classroom?

A short description of the show begins with hopefuls from all over the country gathering for auditions in selected cities. The show's judges choose who will continue in the competition. Selected auditions are aired on the show, some because they are very good and some because they are very bad but very entertaining. (This dichotomy—the show is looking for America's next big

WHY PLAY GAMES?

Young people often avoid mathematics and claim they don't enjoy the subject, yet they are enthusiastic about computer applications or television shows that are clearly based on math. In addition, they might aspire to careers like computer programmer or game designer that will require in-depth study of mathematics. Taking the opportunity to show them that they do math every day, for fun, will go a long way toward breaking down the mental barriers that prevent some students from reaching their potential. And what could be wrong with having a little fun in math class?

ACTIVITY 1: TWEETS THAT GO ON FOREVER AND EVER

Long ago, when dinosaurs walked the earth and telephones were connected to walls by wires, students occasionally launched projects involving chain letters. A student might send a letter to six close friends, asking each of those friends to also send six letters—five to other friends and one to the chain's originator. If all went as planned, the original letter writer would receive a truckload of letters that could be used to demonstrate the power of a geometric progression, and also to perhaps earn a blue ribbon at the mathematics competition.

These projects should have worked in theory, but postage is expensive and it's tiresome to write six letters. Most people broke the chain, so those chain letter projects didn't work very well.

Enter Twitter and Facebook.

It is quick and easy to generate a 140-character tweet that asks friends to pass along a message in order to help out a high school math class. A student who launches yesterday's chain letter project through Twitter will almost certainly get better results. Even better, Twitter offers functionality that will help track that message. A student can count the number of times a tweet has been passed along with a single mouse click on the retweet button. The number of times the person who begins the project is mentioned can be tracked by clicking on the mentions button.

Facebook can be used similarly, by sending messages to Facebook friends and asking them to perform some trackable action, such as posting on the wall of a Facebook page dedicated to the project. Obviously, other social networking sites would also work.

A suggested project plan is presented below, but we encourage you to open a class discussion about ways to augment it. This is an ideal project for collaborative work, and students who are very active on social networks will likely have knowledge of the sites' ever-changing functions that will broaden or focus the project's scope. In addition, we encourage you to be part of the process, either joining one of the groups or working on your own. Delving into the social aspect of the web with your students will be a different experience than your personal social media interactions. You'll get to know them better, and you'll probably learn something.

singing star, but it must be entertaining to get the ratings that keep it on the air—is an interesting topic for class discussion. Mathematics can be brought into the conversation by talking about those ratings, which are available at any time with a quick web search. Did they increase this week? By how much? How can the show's total number of viewers be up when its percentage of the viewership went down?)

The contestants who make the first cut then travel to Hollywood, where they live together during a rehearsal period, and then audition again for the judges. Scenes from the auditions and rehearsals are aired, as well as segments highlighting details from selected contestants' lives. The field is narrowed, again without input from home viewers.

At this point, the more formal competition begins. The show, which airs twice per week at this point, is divided between an evening devoted to competition performances and an evening devoted to reporting the results of those performances. The competition shows often feature a well-known singer who mentors the young competitors on air, as well as mini-interviews with those competitors. The judges watch the performances and offer opinions on the quality of the singing and the presentation, but, and this is key to our discussion, *they do not vote*. Viewers are invited to vote by telephone or by text message during a specified period at the close of the show. On the following night, it is announced who has been eliminated and who will continue in the competition. And this is where the math comes in. Americans vote for their favorite candidates by the millions. The opportunities for classroom activities abound.

There are many websites that attempt to use statistics to corral the tide of information about the *American Idol* competition that is promulgated on the Internet. One prominent site, What Not to Sing! (www.whatnottosing.com), has developed a complex system of sampling viewer feedback at dozens or hundreds of sites each week, and then boiling that feedback down into a system of ratings intended to predict the competition's outcome. An advanced mathematics or statistics class could invest several class periods into dissecting that system and discussing its strengths and weaknesses. (Yes, it samples many sites, but it is unclear that there is a statistically valid way to assign a numerical rating to many individuals' subjective assessments of a performance's quality. On the plus side, the site offers an understandable explanation of standard deviation in a context that might be very interesting to some students (What Not to Sing Team, 2010)).

An interesting look at the interface between *American Idol*, math, and civics could provide some understanding of the ways that our country chooses its leaders. Some questions for classroom discussion might include those listed in Activity 2 at the end of this chapter: "What Can Reality Shows Teach Us About American Electoral Politics?"

Because middle and high school students are almost all too young to vote, watching and participating in activities like *American Idol* can stimulate thinking along the lines of "How much is my vote really worth among the millions cast?" and "I may spend 10 minutes fighting busy signals to register my vote. Do I really want to vote for the cutest boy? Or do I want to vote for the person who deserves to win?" And, of course, with *American Idol*, these students have another factor to consider: "How many times tonight am I willing to vote for this contestant?"

Materials: Computers or other devices capable of accessing Twitter, or the social media site of the teacher's choice; software, such as spreadsheet software, capable of tracking data and generating simple graphs; optional: software capable of fitting a curve to the data generated

Duration: 45 minutes of classroom discussion and project setup; 5 minutes per class period during the project, which can have a duration specified at the teacher's discretion, although we suggest at least 2 weeks

---

Applicable Common Core Standards

Grade 6: Expressions and Equations

Grade 8: Functions

   Expressions and Equations

High School:

   Modeling

Functions: Linear, Quadratic, and Exponential Functions

   Building Functions

Procedure: Divide the class into groups as equal in size as possible. Group them by their preferred social media site, if they have one. (Students who don't use social media will not be at a disadvantage, because the group will be able to use the contacts of the students who do use such sites.)

Introduce the concept of a geometric function by presenting an image of a family tree—an individual has two parents, each of those parents has two parents, and so on with each generation. None of us will ever meet our great-great-great-grandparents, but we all have thirty-two of them. Writing this in terms of a function, with $f(n)$ representing the number of ancestors in a given generation and n representing the number of generations prior to your own (with 0 representing your generation, 1 being your parents' generation, 2 being your grandparents' generation, and so on), we get the following expression:

$$f(n) = 2^n$$

Use this formula to demonstrate the power of the exponential. For example, our great-great-great-grandparents' generation is number 5, and we have 2^5 or 32 great-great-great-grandparents. Our parents' generation is number 1, and we have 2^1 parents, so our formula appears to check out. But look what it tells us—if we go back ten generations, we have 2^{10} or 1,024 great-great-great-great-great-great-great-great-grandparents.

Now, let's move on to Facebook and Twitter. Explain to the class that this new project will use social media to demonstrate the geometric progression's power. Each group will explore this subject in a different way. We suggest a few options below, but we encourage you to allow students to design their own experiments.

Group 1: This group will work with the function we developed during the genealogy discussion: $f(n) = 2^n$. They will select two people from the Facebook (or other social network) friends list and send them a message similar to the following:

> *We're doing a school math project. Would you forward this message to two people on your friends list, and then message us back that you have done so? Thanks!*

This group will track the total number of responses, which should rise exponentially for a while, and then level off and eventually drop to zero, due to nonresponses.

Group 2: This group will send out a message similar to Group 1's message, but they will attempt to track the "generation" of each response, perhaps by adding a counter to the message like this:

> *You are Generation 1. Before forwarding the message, please add one to your generation number.*

With this information, the students should be able to graph their results and compare them to the function $f(n) = 2^n$. We predict that the response will be somewhat less than predicted by the function, because of nonresponses, and that there will also be some unpredictability generated by respondents following the directions incorrectly.

Group 3: This group will explore the true power of the Internet's connectivity. They will all be instructed to message their entire friends lists, asking them to pass along the message to their entire lists and message back that they have done so. If the average student has, say, 200 friends, the potential response can be represented by $f(n) = 200^n$. Nonresponses will surely decrease those numbers, but it will be interesting to see how many responses the effort generates.

Group 4: The previous group assignments were designed with Facebook or similar sites in mind. Place Twitter users in this group and ask them to tweet a request to their lists, asking for a retweet. The results should be similar to Group 3's results, if the number of contacts is similar, but it should be interesting to see whether Twitter's ability to track retweets with a single mouse click makes it more or less cumbersome to track results.

Postactivity Questions

1. Ask students to compile their data, tracking responses over time and, if applicable, by generation. Have them graph their responses and compare them to appropriate geometric functions. Do the results surprise them?
2. Ask students how they would redesign the activity, now that they have seen it in action. Would they change the way they approached potential respondents? Would they change their message? Would they change the site used? Why?
3. What are some other web-related examples of geometric functions? Guide them toward viral videos, which rampage around the world, once a critical number of people decide that their friends just *have* to see this video clip. More sinister are the computer viruses that pass from computer to computer and

proliferate like physical viruses. (Consider teaming with a biology teacher to investigate the mathematics behind the reproduction of the tiny creatures who make us sick.) Can your students come up with other examples? And would they like to take the skills they learned from this project to choose a little-known video and try to make it go viral?

ACTIVITY 2: WHAT CAN REALITY SHOWS TEACH US ABOUT AMERICAN ELECTORAL POLITICS?

For students who are not old enough to register to vote for their president, the opportunity to cast votes for an *American Idol* contestant can loom large as an opportunity to speak up in a world that doesn't usually ask their opinions. This emotional involvement means that questions of statistics they might ordinarily find dry and dull can suddenly be fascinating. The concepts addressed are basic but far-ranging and included in the Common Core Statistics and Probability Standards at all levels.

Capitalize on that increased student interest by asking the following questions.

1. What if the original twenty-four contestants competed, the votes were tallied, and the singer with the most votes took home the prize? Would this necessarily be the person who would win in the current multiple-elimination scenario? Explain some different ways in which the person who is *not* the person preferred by most people could take home the prize.
2. How is the multiple-elimination election process used by *American Idol* similar to our country's system of party primaries? How is it different?
3. What is the effect of allowing individuals to cast multiple votes? Does it measure the intensity of an individual's preference for a particular candidate? Is that a good thing? Does it also give an unfair advantage to people with a lot of time on their hands and unlimited cell or text usage?
4. Consider the election of 2000, in which the electoral votes for the two candidates were so close that the election results were held until the outcome in a single state, Florida, could be decided. In that year, a third party—the Green Party—drew an appreciable number of votes nationwide, including many in Florida. Those votes, if cast for one of the front-running candidates, could have decided the election. Could a similar scenario take place on *American Idol* if more than two contestants were allowed to compete on the final show? Consider, too, the phenomenon represented by the website Vote for the Worst (www.votefortheworst.com). If an appreciable number of people are making a statement about the quality of the contestants by voting for someone who they don't think should win, might that skew the final result?

References

Answers.com. (2010). *American idol*. Answers.com. Retrieved September 24, 2010, from http://www.answers.com/topic/american-idol#Television_ratings.
BBC Productions USA (Producer). (2003). *What not to wear*. New York: Discovery Channel & The Learning Channel.

BBC Worldwide (Creator). (2005). *Dancing with the stars*. New York: ABC.

Broome, D. (Creator). (2004). *The biggest loser*. New York: NBC.

Bunim, M. E. (Producer), & Murray, J. (Producer). (1992). *The real world*. New York: MTV.

Collins, S. (2009). American Idol tracker blog entry. *The Los Angeles Times*. Retrieved August 15, 2010, from http://latimesblogs.latimes.com/americanidoltracker/2009/05/american-idol-ended-its-eighth-season-last-week-so-what-will-fans-do-with-all-this-newfound-free-time-why-delve-into-anoth.html.

Common Core State Standards Initiative. (2010). *Common Core State Standards for English language arts & literacy in history/social studies, science, and technical subjects*. Washington, DC: National Governors Association Center for Best Practices and the Council of Chief State School Officers.

Endemol (Producer). (2003). *Extreme makeover: Home edition*. New York: ABC.

Fuller, S. (Producer). (2002). *American idol*. New York: Fox Broadcasting Company.

Funt, A. (Producer). (1948). *Candid camera*. New York: ABC.

Gross, D. (2010). Dictionary word of the year: 'Unfriend.' *CNN*. Retrieved August 15, 2010, from http://www.cnn.com/2009/TECH/11/17/unfriend.word/index.html.

Halaban, B. (Director). (2002). *While you were out*. New York: The Learning Channel.

Kutcher, A. (Producer), & Goldberg, J. (Producer). (2003). *Punk'd*. New York: MTV.

Langley, J. (Producer), & Barbour, M. (Producer). (1989). *COPS*. New York: Fox.

Maxis (Developer). (2000). *The Sims*. Redwood City, CA: Electronic Arts.

Maxis (Developer), & Nintendo EAD (Developer). (1989). *SimCity*. Redwood City, CA: Electronic Arts.

MicroProse (Developer). (1999). *Rollercoaster tycoon*. Alameda, CA: Hasbro Interactive.

Murphy, S. (2010). Teens ditch e-mail for texting and Facebook. *TechNewsDaily*. Retrieved August 15, 2010, from http://www.msnbc.msn.com/id/38585236/ns/technology_and_science-tech_and_gadgets/.

O'Toole, M. (2011). Merriam-Webster dictionary adds "tweet," "bromance," "fist bump." *Reuters*. Retrieved August 26, 2011, from http://www.reuters.com/article/2011/08/25/us-dictionary-words-idUSTRE77O6I420110825.

Taylor, J. (Producer). (2002). *The Osbournes*. New York: MTV.

What Not to Sing Team. (2010). Homepage. *What not to sing!* Retrieved August 15, 2010, from http://www.whatnottosing.com.

Zynga (Developer). (2009). *FarmVille*. San Francisco, CA: Zynga.

CONCLUSION

Literacy skills and mathematical understanding are indispensible tools for living in our society, in and of themselves. It is our belief that, taken together, literacy skills enhance mathematical understanding, and it is our hope that we have given the readers of this book a toolkit of teaching strategies capable of reaching all students. Mathematics explains the way our universe works, and language is the tool we use to explain the universe to each other. Use them to open a new world for your students . . . then another . . . then another . . .

APPENDIX A

Selections from *Artifacts*

PROLOGUE

There is no record of the name that the island's native inhabitants gave their home. The Spanish paused there only long enough to kill and plunder. Any name they gave it did not survive. The French stayed long enough to christen it appropriately—Isle Dernier. The English, though accomplished at empire-building, were not original thinkers. They merely translated the French name into their own tongue, and English-speaking Americans never knew the island by any name other than Last Isle.

Nature was never kind to Last Isle. It was inundated by hurricanes time and again; each storm surge trenched further through the land, leaving it broken into pieces that over time acquired names of their own. Some of those pieces can no longer even be called islands.

Around the turn of the twentieth century, cartographers renamed the remains of Last Isle to acknowledge their plurality. Current sea charts no longer show a Last Isle. Instead, they warn mariners wishing to explore the crystalline waters off the Florida Panhandle to beware treacherous shallows around the Last Isles.

Long ago, life on Last Isle was idyllic. Its natives had no need of agriculture, given its abundance of fish and shellfish and waterfowl. Unfortunately, people whose lives are easy attract the attention of people whose lives are not. Their isolation had long protected the people of Last Isle from invasion, but the barrier of distance fell before the European conquerors in their tall ships. When they arrived, the massacres began in earnest.

Long before the Americans finally wrested West Florida—and Last Isle with it—from the Spanish, the massacres had tapered off. There was no one left to kill. Then the slavers auctioned their human wares to the planters and misery came again to Last Isle. It took a great war to end the misery and even tiny, remote Last Isle was touched by that war. Only humans, among all nature's creatures, could contemplate death in the midst of the island's primeval beauty. Its old trees have watched over centuries of killing, but they do not understand it yet.

The Last Isles are even now an attractive haven for a killer looking for a place to conceal a crime. No witnesses to murder lurk there, so far from civilization. There could be no more convenient place to rid oneself of an inconvenient corpse. With such a history, it is not surprising that the past and its bones sometimes surface there. It would be more surprising if they did not.

CHAPTER 1 OF *ARTIFACTS*

Faye Longchamp was digging like a pothunter and she hated herself for it. Pothunters were a bare notch above graverobbers. They were vultures. Once a pothunter defiled an ancient site, archaeologists could only hope to salvage a fraction of the information it had once held. And information, not artifacts, was the goal of legitimate archaeology.

Pothunters, on the other hand, only sought artifacts with a hefty street value, and to hell with egg-headed academics who condemned them for trashing history as they dug. There was no more precise description of what she was doing; therefore, she had sunk to the level of a pothunter. The fact that she was desperate for cold, hard cash did not absolve her.

A narrow beach to her left and a sparse stand of sea oats to her right were all that stood between Faye and the luminous turquoise of the Gulf of Mexico. Since pothunters couldn't excavate in the open, in front of God and everybody, they worked in places like this, patches of sand too small to have names. Not a soul lived in the Last Isles, and the island chain paralleled a thinly populated stretch of Florida Panhandle coastline. It was a good place to do work that shouldn't be seen.

Looking up from her lucrative but illegal hobby, she glanced furtively over her shoulder at Seagreen Island. Its silhouette loomed like a dark whale cresting in the distance.

She knew how to excavate properly. During her abortive college career, she had tried to learn everything about field technique that her idol, Dr. Magda Stockard, could teach her. Even ten years later, working as she did on Seagreen Island as a field supervisor under Magda's watchful eye, she still learned something new every day. And she loved it. She loved sifting soil samples through a quarter-inch mesh and cataloging the seeds, beads, and bones that stayed behind. She loved the fact that every day was a treasure hunt. She would have worked for free, if she could have ignored her pesky need for food and shelter. The paycheck she received for painstaking work performed amid the heat and the humidity and the mosquitoes was always welcome, but it was insufficient.

Her work on Seagreen Island was legitimate, but it disturbed her nonetheless. Unless Magda's archaeological survey turned up a culturally significant site, there would be nothing to stop the developers who wanted to build a resort there. The lush and tangled vegetation topping the island would be scraped off to make room for a hotel and tennis courts and a spa and a couple of swimming pools. As if Florida needed more swimming pools.

This islet where she stood was too tiny to interest developers, though the government had found it worth including in a national wildlife refuge. It was really no more than a sandbar sprinkled with scrubby vegetation, but Faye's instincts had always been reliable. The Last Isles were once awash in wealth. The wind and waves couldn't have carried it all away; they must have left some of it under the sand, ripe for discovery by a needy pothunter. A tiny bit of that dead glory would pay this year's property taxes. A big, valuable chunk of the past would save her home forever.

Home. The thought of losing her home made Faye want to hurl her trowel to the ground in frustration, but doing so would require her to stop digging and she couldn't do that. Something in her blood would never let her quit digging. Faye did not intend to be the one who let the family down.

***

Two eager archaeology students had volunteered to stay behind the rest of their field crew on mosquito-infested Seagreen Island. Tomorrow would have been soon enough to catalog the day's finds and mark the next swath of dig spots, but these two were too dedicated to their work for their own good. If the student archaeologists had cleared out on the stroke of five, they could have been enjoying Tuesday-night sitcoms and beer with their colleagues. Instead, they were conscientiously digging their own graves.

The sun kept sliding toward the Gulf of Mexico, and the red-haired woman kept squinting through the viewfinder of her surveyor's transit. She barked directions to her partner as he slowly—so slowly—placed one flag after another in yet another nice neat row. They checked and rechecked the grid of sampling spots, careful to ensure that everything was exactly as their supervisor had recorded in the field notebook that the young woman clutched like a bible.

The young man twisted the surveyor's flag, yelling, "Hey, Krista, there's so many roots here, I can hardly get it in the ground."

The young man grunted as he pushed the flag into the soil, ignorant of what lay beneath his feet. The base probed deeper. It struck something horrible, but the young man and his companion remained unaware, so they were allowed to continue breathing.

***

Faye knelt at the edge of the evening's excavation. She'd put in a full day on Seagreen Island. Then, after her colleagues' boat was safely out of sight, she'd worked nearly another half-day here. It seemed like she had displaced half the little islet's soil and her biceps quivered from the strain. She had been so sure. Her instincts had screamed, "This is the spot," the moment she dragged her skiff onto the bedraggled beach. This was a place for buried treasure, a place to dig up the find that would change her life. She still felt that electric anticipation, but her shovel had turned over nothing but sand.

The aluminum-on-sand groan of Joe's flat-bottomed johnboat being dragged onto the beach caught her ear, but his presence didn't disturb her dogged work. She hardly looked up when he said, "It's about dark, Faye. If you ain't already found anything worth digging up, you won't be finding it tonight."

Joe was right, so she ignored him.

He tried again. "Faye, the day's gone. Come home and eat some supper. You can try again tomorrow."

Faye continued to ignore him.

Joe sighed, glanced at the last scrap of sun melting into the Gulf and squatted on his haunches beside her. "Okay, you want to dig in the dark? Let's dig in the dark. You got another one of those little hand-shovel things?"

Faye could steel herself against displaying her emotions, even on occasions when outbursts were expected. At funerals, Faye was the competent one who made sure that the other mourners had comfortable chairs and fresh handkerchiefs. She grieved later, alone in her car, undone by the sight of a woman sitting at the bus stop with her head cocked at her mother's angle.

Sometimes, when forced to carry on long past any sane person's breaking point, she found herself weeping at dog food commercials. Now, since she no longer had a TV, she was denied even that cheap outlet, so she was defenseless in the face of Joe's chivalrous offer. The sudden tears surprised her.

"Why are you crying? Don't do that!" Joe cried.

Faye, in her state of emotional upheaval, found Joe's panicked squeak uproarious. She plopped to the ground, laughing.

Joe bent over her with his brow furrowed in confusion and demanded, "Why are you laughing? What's wrong?"

"I'm laughing because you think I'm an idiot for digging in the dark, but you're willing to be an idiot, too, rather than leave me alone with the sand fleas."

Joe put his hand on her shoulder. His solicitous tone did nothing to quench her giggles. "And why are you crying?"

Her giggles subsided. "Because you're the best friend I ever had."

Joe brushed his ponytail over his shoulder and looked at the few stars bright enough to penetrate the early evening haze. "Aw, Faye. Smart, pretty girl like you—you're bound to have bunches of friends."

"No, not many. You don't know how hard it is…." She swallowed the suggestion that Joe wouldn't understand how hard life could be for a child who wasn't really white or black, who didn't fit neatly into any racial pigeonhole at all, because she knew better. The bronze tint of the skin over his high cheekbones said that Joe Wolf Mantooth knew all about it.

Whether he knew what she was thinking or just sensed it was time to change the subject, Joe took the trowel from her hand. Humming in his monotone way, he aimlessly moved soil around the bottom of the pit Faye had excavated. They both heard the muted click when the trowel struck something that wasn't rock, nor metal, nor plastic. On their hands and knees immediately, they saw the object at once. It was the color of the sand that nearly buried it, but its sleek, gleaming curve attracted the eye. Faye, instinctively falling back on her archaeological training, reached into her back pocket for a fine paintbrush to work the sand gently away from the surface of this human skull.

Joe jumped up, saying, "We have to go home and get my stuff, Faye. There's a lot of things I need to do."

Joe believed in the old ways from his skin-clad feet to his pony-tailed head and Faye respected his desire to consecrate this old grave. He fumbled in the large leather pouch that always hung from his belt. "I've got tobacco here, but nothing else. I need to go home and get some food, and a clay pot to put it in. And some coals from my fire and some cleansing herbs for washing. Faye—"

Faye held up a hand for him to be quiet, because she was busy assessing the skull's archaeological context. It was unusual to find a burial like this one, unassociated with other graves or signs of human habitation, but it wasn't a complete aberration. She'd read that Choctaw warriors killed in battle were buried by their wives on the very spot where they fell. The burial had to be accomplished without disturbing the corpse, without even touching it. As Faye brushed sand away from a sizeable fracture radiating from the skull's temple, she wondered whether she was the first person to touch this man since his killer had bashed his brains out.

"Faye, let's go. This guy's rested here a long time and we've disturbed him. We got to help him rest again. It's the right thing to do. It ain't respectful to wait."

Faye didn't answer Joe, because she was busy. She would discuss this with him in a minute; he'd just have to be patient with her. She was wholeheartedly glad he knew how to treat this burial with respect. She may have become a common pothunter, but she was no graverobber and disturbing the dead chilled her bones. Joe's makeshift funeral rites assuaged her guilt a bit.

Still, she wished that he would hush for just a minute while she examined this skull.

***

The cabbage palms of Seagreen Island cast jagged shadows on the red-haired girl's face as she initialed her field notebook with a flourish. She ran her fingers through an inch-long crop of spiky hair.

"Done," she said. "I can't believe we finished before dark."

"Dr. Stockard would probably say 'Quick work is imprecise work.'"

"I don't care," was the girl's airy reply. "Let's go check the sample bags so we can eat supper and go to bed."

They crossed the crest of the small hill that ran down the spine of Seagreen Island. In their wake stood a tidy row of surveyor's flags, each consisting of a simple length of wire topped with a rectangle of orange vinyl. The flags marched straight toward a mammoth live oak tree and the last one stood in the shade of the oak's moss-draped branches.

Early the next morning, the rest of the field crew would arrive to dig a test pit at each spot marked by a flag. If they were to dig under the live oak, their shovels would turn over more than just dirt.

***

Faye picked up a twig and rested it on the bone that had once underlain somebody's upper lip. She tried to slide it into the skull's former nostril, but the twig butted up against a bony ridge.

"You're off the hook, Joe. There's no need for any mystic tobacco-and-corn ceremony. This is a Caucasian skull. I'll just cover him up and say a Christian prayer over him. If he was a European invader of the rape-and-pillage variety, even my puny prayer would be too good for him."

Faye traced her fingertips over the soil surface, looking for artifacts she might have disturbed while digging, and was rewarded with a clod of soil that was too heavy for its size. She worked the dirt away from the solid center of the clod while she listened to Joe argue his point.

"Everybody deserves a comfortable grave, Faye. Just let me go get my—"

Somewhere in the direction of Seagreen Island, Faye heard a boat motor turn over. Pointing at the sound, she barked, "Help me cover her up. Somebody's coming."

Joe tended to obey authoritative voices, so he dropped his argument and began shoveling dirt back into the excavation, but he didn't stop talking. "Why did you say 'her?' I thought you said 'him' before. How do you know that this was a girl?"

Faye kept shoving dirt over the skull without answering Joe. Getting caught would be an outright disaster. First, she was digging in a national wildlife preserve and removing archaeological materials from federal lands was a felony. Second, a brush with the law—and the fines and legal expenses that would accompany such trouble—would hasten the inevitable loss of her home. And third, the artifact in her hand suggested that she might be treading on legal quicksand far more serious than simple pothunting.

As they sprinted toward their boats, she held out her hand to show Joe the single item she had removed from the grave. "This is how I knew she was a girl."

A corroded pearl dangled from an ornate diamond-studded platinum earring. Her practiced eye saw that it was machine-made and recent, but no archaeological knowledge was required to date this artifact. Any woman alive who ever played in her mother's jewelry box could guess its age. The delicate screw-back apparatus dated it to the mid-twentieth century and the style pinpointed the period still further. The woman who wore this earring had wished very much to look like Jackie Kennedy.

Somebody had buried her in a spot where she was unlikely to ever be found. Most likely, that somebody had killed her.

***

Walking up the wooden stairs and onto the broad porch of her home never failed to settle Faye's soul. Even tonight, after violating her professional ethics, breaking several laws, and disturbing the dead, she was soothed by the gentle sea breeze that blew through the open front door.

The old house and its island had both been named Joyeuse by one of Faye's ancestors whose name she didn't know. The old plantation house on Joyeuse Island was more than home to her. It was a treasure entrusted to her by her mother and her grandmother and her grandmother's mother and, most of all, by her great-great-grandmother Cally, the former slave who had somehow come to own the remnants of a great plantation.

Cally's story was lost to time. No one remembered how a woman of color had acquired Joyeuse Island and held onto it for seventy years, but Cally had done it, and her descendants had preserved her legacy and her bloodline. Something of Cally lived on in Faye, maybe in her dark eyes or her darker hair, but another, essential, part of Cally survived in the home she fought to keep. Joyeuse was a decrepit relic of antebellum plantation culture, built by human beings laboring for people who believed they owned them. Even so, it was a calm, beautiful place and Faye had learned to live with the ambiguity of that. Sometimes Faye thought Ambiguity should have been her middle name.

If race is the abiding conflict of the Americas, then Faye considered herself the physical embodiment of that conflict. Her great-great-grandmother Cally had been born a slave on Joyeuse plantation, the product of the master's assault on her mother. Unprovable family lore said that the master himself was not as white as he might have thought; his grandmother was half-Creek. There were surely people who died on the Trail of Tears with no more Native American blood than he.

Faye's ancestors had sprung from Europe and the Americas and Africa and God-knew-where-else. The casual observer, noting her darker-than-olive skin, tiny build, delicate features, and stick-straight black hair, would be hard-pressed to name her racial affiliation. Faye was never too sure herself.

Settling herself on a ramshackle porch swing, she studied the earring in her hand. She couldn't call the law. How would she explain why she was digging on Federal land?

Faye tucked one foot under her and pushed against the floor's cypress boards with the other, ever careful to maintain her balance. How many times in her childhood had she leaned back too far and felt the old swing dump her onto her head? Then, once she'd learned the trick, how many times had she done it on purpose because it was fun to fall, heels over ears, into a giggling heap of little girl? All those memories would be sand under the feet of anyone but Faye. There was no way in hell she was going to let Joyeuse go.

She swung herself gently back and forth. What harm would it do to forget she'd ever seen those bones? One more good hurricane and they would be swept away, anyway. She hated to think about someone getting away with murder but, in reality, someone already had. What was the likelihood that a critical clue had survived for decades under damp, wet sand? Still, her sense of right and wrong said that she ought to tell somebody. The dead woman's family would derive some comfort in knowing, with certainty, that she was never coming home.

Her sense of self-preservation wouldn't let her go to the police, but her conscience wasn't quite ready to let her destroy evidence of a murder. Keeping the earring at least gave her the option of doing the right thing someday. But where could she hide the evidence? There was no available nook in Joyeuse's above-ground basement; she knew that. It was built of tabby, a durable concrete concocted of oyster shells, lime, and sand, and it would survive a direct atomic strike. After more than a hundred and fifty years, there were still no crevices large enough to serve as a hiding place in its rock-like surface.

She climbed the staircase tucked under the back porch roof, leaving the service rooms in the basement behind. The main floor sat a full story above ground level, a form of house design that was prudent in a hurricane zone. Faye wandered around the main floor, poking around in the ladies' parlor and the gentlemen's parlor and the vast room that had served as both dining room and ballroom. The fine furnishings and draperies were long-gone and the cavernous empty chambers offered no nook to house the old pearl earring. There was really only one place in the whole house that offered hiding places that she didn't already use to store her everyday necessities, and it was two stories above her.

She climbed the porch staircase to the next level, which had housed the bedchambers and music room back when the house served as a home for a large family and its servants. She'd converted the two largest bedrooms into her temple to legitimate archaeology, two treasure rooms where she stored artifacts that made her black-market customers sneer.

The walls of her own bedroom and the adjacent master bedroom were lined with glass-fronted shelves loaded with unsalable finds. Cracked pottery, broken bone tools, the bones and shell of a turtle—the discovery of each of these things was described in waterproof ink on the pages of the field notebooks stacked on the topmost shelf. Any of these shelves could have served as a hiding place for the earring, but Faye had another spot in mind. She reached in a broom closet for a long-handled implement tipped with a metal hook, but before she could use it, she heard Joe coming.

Faye listened to Joe climbing the spiral staircase that rose through the precise center of the old house, piercing the square landing that provided access to the rooms on this level. Joe's footfalls were quiet and fast. The ordinary listener wouldn't have heard him coming. His moccasined feet made no percussive tap as they hit the treads, but there was a faint creaking in the old wood that Faye, attuned to any disturbance in her cherished home, couldn't ignore.

Joe rose through the floor and stepped onto the landing, saying, "I made something for you, Faye. I was saving it for later, but I think you've had a hard day."

She took Joe's gift and turned it over in her hands, unable to think of an appropriate response other than, "You shouldn't have gone to so much trouble for me."

The workmanship couldn't be criticized. Joe was very, very clever with his hands. There was no way to tell him that it was wrong to alter something thousands of years old; she didn't intend to try.

Joe had used new materials to reconstruct fragments of an *atlatl* made by West Florida's Deptford people before the birth of Christ. Starting with a stone weight and a shell trigger that he'd taken from her display case, Joe had whittled and chipped the missing pieces of the *atlatl*, an archaic type of spear that was thrown by slinging its hinged spearthrower in a whiplash motion. The crowning glory of Joe's gift was a finely flaked stone point crafted out of chert, the same native stone Florida's original inhabitants had used in their tools. Given his penchant for stone tools and homemade glue, she couldn't hazard a guess as to how much of Joe's time she held in her hands. There was nothing Faye could do but thank him sincerely and resolve to keep her artifact cases locked in the future.

Joe, embarrassed by the encounter, disappeared down the stairs. Faye hefted the *atlatl*, choosing a prominent place for it in a display case in her bedroom, then she lifted the hooked tool above her head. It grabbed hold of a recessed ring in the ceiling and she pulled hard. A hidden trap door opened, and she unfolded the rickety wooden ladder that dangled from the door. This was why she rarely ventured into Joyeuse's cupola. It was so dang hard to get up there.

Once she had struggled up through the trapdoor, she saw the cranny she'd had in mind. By standing on a windowsill and stretching upward, she could reach her hand into a gap between the top of the wall and the rafters. It was the perfect hiding place….

…And someone had found it before. There was a wooden box there, about the size of a shoebox, and she gingerly lifted it down to her eye level. Aside from an inch-thick layer of matted dust, the box was in good shape. Carefully dovetailed together without a visible nail, the box itself was an exciting find. She tucked the earring atop a rafter and sat down to study the box.

Faye knew how Howard Carter must have felt, clearing rubble day after day from the staircase leading to King Tut's tomb, knowing that wonderful things awaited him, but savoring the anticipation. She hefted the box in her hands a moment—it wasn't empty, she could tell—then she lifted the lid and her breath left her.

It was an old book bound in leather and canvas, and handwritten across the cover were the words, "Journal of Wm. Whitehall, begun on May 15, 1782, to commemorate the Birth of his Daughter, Mariah." William Whitehall had formed each "*f*" with a long, vertical curve shaped like an "*s*." Time wrought changes in everything, even the alphabet, and that sometimes made manuscripts of this age devilish to interpret.

The penmanship made Faye think of John Hancock's unrepentant signature on the Declaration of Independence, and her breath left her again. A man who was an adult in 1782 was a contemporary of John Hancock and his revolutionary friends.

The journal was stuffed full of stray sheets of paper. A palm-sized portrait of a man in a powdered wig slipped free and drifted toward the dusty floor, but Faye, who had the instincts of a museum curator, caught it without so much as crinkling the yellowed paper.

She opened the journal and saw that William, like others of a time when paper was hard to come by, had inscribed each page in the normal left-to-right fashion, then turned the book a quarter-turn to the right and written another full page of text atop the first. No wonder neat penmanship was so valued in those days. It was going to take her quite awhile to decipher what William had to tell her.

Excerpt from the journal of William Whitehall, May 15, 1782

My Woman—that is to say my Wife, for we are as Married as two people can be in the absence of proper Clergy—demonstrated true courage today, whilst I cower'd in the meadow alone, except for my pipe & my tobacco. After the hard labour of the day had been done by others, I stood—hat in hand—outside my own home and humbly begged permission to enter in. The Creek midwife acknowledged my presence with a bare nod, as is her way, and I stumbled into a house of miracles. As I thanked the Almighty for this hale and healthy Child, that most precious of gifts, the Sun lay lightly on my Susan's flush'd cheeks, and she lifted the Infant toward me so gently, so slightly, that the motion was hardly visible. I seized the invitation & I seized the child. "A girl," my Susan murmur'd. I would have known the Baby was female merely by the shape of her dainty face.

I search'd that face, endeavouring to assess the shape of the eyes, the colour of the skin, tho' unaware that I did it. Then Susan, who has attended the births of Creeks and of Whites and of Half-breeds like herself, said, "All Babies look the same, puffy and red. After a time, you will see whether she looks like you or like me, but you will have to wait." She looked strait in my eyes & I was shamed.

APPENDIX B

A Concordance of the Words Used in the Opening Passages of *Artifacts* by Mary Anna Evans

& 1, 15, 1782, a, aberration, abiding, abortive, about, above-ground, absence, absolve, abundance, academics, access, accompany, accomplished, acknowledge, acquired, across, adjacent, adult, affiliation, Africa, after, again, against, age, ago, agriculture, aimlessly, ain't, airy, alive, all, allowed, Almighty, alone, alphabet, already, alter, aluminum-on-sand, always, ambiguity, American, amid, among, an, ancestors, ancient, and, angle, another, answer, answering, antebellum, anticipation, any, anyone, anything, anyway, apparatus, appropriate, archaeological, archaeologists, archaeology, archaic, are, argue, argument, around, arrive, arrived, artifact, artifacts, as, aside, assault, assess, assessing, assuaged, at, atlatl, atomic, atop, attended, attention, attract, attracted, attractive, attuned, auctioned, authoritative, available, aw, awaited, awash, away, awhile, babies, baby, back, bags, balance, ballroom, bare, barked, barrier, base, basement, bashed, battle, be, beach, beads, beautiful, beauty, because, become, bed, bedchambers, bedraggled, bedroom, bedrooms, been, beer, before, began, begged, begun, behind, being, beings, believe, believed, belt, beneath, bent, beside, best, better, between, beware, bible, biceps, big, birth, births, bit, black, black-market, blew, blood, bloodline, boards, boat, boats, bone, bones, bony, book, born, both, bottom, bound, box, brains, branches, breaking, breath, breathing, breeze, bright, broad, broken, bronze, broom, brow, brush, brushed, build, built, bunches, burial, buried, bus, busy, but, butted, by, cabbage, call, called, Cally, Cally's, calm, came, can, can't, canvas, car, care, career, careful, carefully, carried, carry, Carter, cartographers, case, cases, cash, cast, casual, catalog, cataloging, Caucasian, caught, cavernous, ceiling, center, centuries, century, ceremony, certainty, chain, chairs, chambers, change, changes, chapter, charts, cheap, check, checked, cheekbones, cheeks, cherished, chert, child, childhood, chilled, chipped, chivalrous, Choctaw, choosing, Christ, christen, Christian, chunk, civilization, clay, cleansing, cleared, clearing, clergy, clever, click, climbed, climbing, clod, closet, clue, clutched, coals, coastline, cocked, cold, colleagues, college, color, colour, come, comfort, comfortable, coming, commemorate, commercials, common, companion, competent, complete, conceal, concocted, concrete, condemned, conflict, confusion, conquerors, conscience, conscientiously, consecrate, considered, consisting, contemplate, contemporary, context, continue, continued, convenient, converted, corpse, corroded, could, couldn't, couple, courage, courts, cover, cower'd, cracked, crafted, cranny, creaking, creatures, Creek, Creeks, crest, cresting, crevices, crew, cried, crime, crinkling, critical, criticized, crop, crossed, crowning, crying, crystalline, culturally, culture, cupola, curator, current, curve, customers, cypress, dainty, damp, dang, dangled, dark, darker, darker-than-olive, date, dated, daughter, day, day's, days, dead, death, decades, decipher, Declaration, decrepit, dedicated, deeper, defenseless, defiled, delicate, demanded, demonstrated, denied, Deptford, derive, Dernier, descendants, described, description, deserves, design, desire, desperate, destroy, developers, devilish, diamond-studded, did, died, dig, digging, dining, direct, direction, directions, dirt, disappeared, disaster, discovery, discuss, displaced, display, displaying, distance, disturb, disturbance, disturbed, disturbing, do, dog, dogged, doing, don't, done, door, dovetailed, down, Dr., dragged, draperies, drifted, dropped, dug, dump, durable, during, dust, dusty, each, eager, ear, early, earnest, earring, ears, easy, eat, edge, egg-headed, electric, else, embarrassed, embodiment, emotional, emotions, empire-building, empty, encounter, end, endeavouring, English, English-speaking, enjoying, enough, ensure, enter, entrusted, essential, ethics, Europe, European, even, evening, evening's, ever, every, everybody, everyday, everything, evidence, exactly, examined, excavate, excavated, excavation, except, excerpt, exciting, expected, expenses, explain, explore, eye, eyes, "f", face, fact, failed, faint, fall, falling, family, fashion, fast, Faye, Faye's, features, federal, feet, fell, felony, felt, female, few, field, fifty, finally, find, finding, finds, fine, finely, fines, fingers, fingertips, finished, fire, first, fish, fit, five, flag, flags, flaked, flat-bottomed, fleas, floor, floor's, Florida, Florida's, flourish, flush'd, food, foot, footfalls, for, forced, forever, forget, form, formed, former, forth, fought, found, fraction, fracture, fragments, free, French, fresh, friend, friends, from, front, frustration, full, fumbled, fun, funeral, funerals, furnishings, furrowed, further, furtively, future, gap, gave, gentle, gentlemen's, gently, get, getting, gift, gifts, giggles, giggling, gingerly, girl, girl's, given, glad, glanced, glass-fronted, gleaming, glory, glue, go, goal, God, God-knew-where-else, going, gone, good, got, government, grabbed, grandmother, grandmother's, grave, graverobber, graverobbers, graves, great, great-great-grandmother, grid, grieved, groan, ground, grunted, guess, guilt, Gulf, guy's, habitation, had, hair, hale, half, half-breeds, half-Creek, half-day, Hancock, Hancock's, hand, handkerchiefs, hands, hand-shovel, handwritten, hard, hardly, hard-pressed, harm, has, hasten, hated, haunches, have, haven, hazard, haze, he, he'd, head, healthy, heap, heard, heat, heavy, heels, hefted, hefty, held, hell, help, her, herbs, here, herself, hey, hidden, hide, hiding, high, hill, him, himself, hinged, his, history, hit, hobby, hold, home, homemade, hook, hooked, hope, horrible, hotel, house, housed, how, Howard, human, humans, humbly, humidity, humming, hundred, hung, hunt, hurl, hurricane, hurricanes, hush, I, I'll, I'm, I've, idiot, idol, idyllic, if, ignorant, ignore, ignored, illegal, immediately, implement, imprecise, in, inch-long, inch-thick, including, inconvenient, Independence, inevitable, infant, information, inhabitants, initialed, ink, inscribed, Instead, instinctively, instincts, insufficient, intend, interest, interpret, into, inundated, invader, invasion, invitation, is, island, island's, islands, Isle, Isles, islet, islet's, isolation, it, it's, item, its, itself, Jackie, jagged, jewelry, Joe, Joe's, John, johnboat, journal, Joyeuse, Joyeuse's, jumped, just, keep, keeping, Kennedy, kept, kill, killed, killer, killing, kind, king, knees, knelt, knew, know, knowing, knowledge, known, Krista, laboring, labour, ladder, ladies', land, landing, lands, large, largest, Last, later, laughing, law, laws, lay, layer, leading, leaned, learn, learned, least, leather, leave, leaving, left, left-to-right, legacy, legal, legitimate, length, let, let's, level, lid, life, lifted, lightly, like, likelihood, likely, lime, lined, lip, listened, listener, little, live, lived, lives, loaded, locked, long, Longchamp, longer, long-gone, long-handled, look, looked, looking, looks, loomed, lore, losing, loss, lost, lot, loved, lucrative, luminous, lurk, lush, machine-made, made, Magda, Magda's, main, maintain, make, makeshift, mammoth, man, Mantooth, manuscripts, many, marched, Mariah, mariners, mark, marked, married, massacres, master, master's, materials, matted, may, maybe, me, meadow, melting, memories, merely, mesh, metal, Mexico, middle, midst, mid-twentieth, midwife, might, mind, minute, miracles, misery, missing, moccasined, moment, monotone, more, morning, mosquitoes, mosquito-infested, moss-draped, Most, mother, mother's, motion, motor, mourners, moved, much, murder, murmur'd, museum, music, must, muted, my, mystic, nail, name, named, names, narrow, national, native, natives, Nature, nature's, nearly, neat, neatly, necessities, need, needed, needy, never, new, next, nice, no, nod, nonetheless, nook, nor, normal, nostril, not, notch, notebook, notebooks, nothing, noting, now, oak, oak's, oats, obey, object, observer, occasions, of, off, offer, offered, okay, old, on, once, one, oneself, only, onto, open, opened, option, or, orange, ordinary, original, ornate, other, others, ought, out, outbursts, outlet, outright, over, own, owned, oyster, page, painstaking, paintbrush, palms, palm-sized, Panhandle, panicked, paper, paralleled, parlor, part, partner, past, patches, patient, paused, pay, paycheck, pearl, penchant, penetrate, penmanship, people, percussive, perfect, performed, period, permission, person, person's, pesky, physical, picked, pieces, piercing, pigeonhole, pinpointed, pipe, pit, place, placed, places, plantation, planters, plastic, platinum, played, plopped, plunder, plurality, pocket, point, pointing, poking, police, ponytail, pony-tailed, pools, populated, porch, portrait, pot, pothunter, pothunters, pothunting, pottery, pouch, powdered, practiced, prayer, precious, precise, presence, preserve, preserved, pretty, primeval, probably, probed, product, professional, prologue, prominent, proper, properly, property, protected, provided, prudent, puffy, pulled, puny, purpose, pushed, put, quarter-inch, quench, quick, quicksand, quiet, quit, quite, quivered, race, racial, radiating, rafter, rafters, ramshackle, ran, rape-and-pillage, rarely, rather, reach, reached, read, ready, reality, really, received, recent, recessed, rechecked, reconstruct, record, recorded, rectangle, red, red-haired, refuge, reliable, relic, remained, remains, remembered, remnants, remote, removed, removing, renamed, reply, require, required, resolve, resort, respect, respected, respectful, response, rest, rested, revolutionary, rewarded, rickety, rid, ridge, right, ring, ripe, rites, rock, rock-like, roof, room, rooms, roots, rose, row, rubble, "s", safely, said, salvage, same, sample, samples, sampling, sand, sandbar, sane, sat, save, saving, savoring, saw, say, saying, scrap, scraped, screamed, screw-back, scrubby, sea, Seagreen, search'd, second, see, seeds, seemed, seen, seized, self-preservation, sense, sensed, serious, servants, serve, served, service, settle, settling, seventy, several, shade, shadows, shallows, shamed, shape, shaped, she, she'd, sheets, shelf, shell, shellfish, shells, shelter, shelves, ships, shoebox, should, shoulder, shouldn't, shovel, shoveling, shovels, shoving, show, sifting, sighed, sight, signature, significant, signs, silhouette, simple, since, sincerely, single, sitcoms, site, sitting, size, sizeable, skiff, skin, skinclad, skull, slave, slavers, sleek, slide, sliding, slightly, slinging, slipped, slowly, small, smart, sneer, so, soil, solicitous, solid, some, somebody, somebody's, someday, somehow, someone, something, sometimes, somewhere, soon, soothed, sought, soul, sound, spa, Spanish, sparse, spear, spearthrower, spiky, spine, spiral, spot, spots, sprinkled, sprinted, sprung, square, squatted, squeak, squinting, stacked, staircase, stairs, stand, standing, stars, starting, state, stay, stayed, steel, stepped, stick-straight, still, Stockard, stone, stood, stop, store, stored, stories, storm, story, straight, strain, strait, stray, street, stretch, stretching, strike, stroke, struck, struggled, student, students, studied, study, stuff, stuffed, stumbled, style, subject, subsided, such, sudden, suggested, suggestion, sun, sunk, supervisor, supper, sure, surely, surface, surge, surprised, surprising, survey, surveyor's, survive, survived, Susan, Susan's, swallowed, swath, swept, swimming, swing, swung, tabby, take, taken, talking, tall, tangled, tap, tapered, taxes, teach, tears, technique, tell, temple, ten, tended, tennis, test, text, than, thank, thanked, that, the, their, them, then, there, there's, therefore, these, they, thing, things, think, thinkers, thinking, thinly, third, this, tho', those, though, thousands, through, thrown, tidy, time, times, tint, tiny, tipped, to, tobacco, tobacco-and-corn, today, together, tomb, tomorrow, tone, tongue, tonight, too, took, tool, tools, top, topmost, topped, topping, touch, touched, touching, toward, traced, trail, training, transit, translated, trap, trapdoor, trashing, treacherous, treading, treads, treasure, treat, tree, trees, trenched, trick, tried, trigger, trouble, trowel, true, try, tucked, Tuesday-night, turn, turned, turquoise, Tut's, TV, twentieth, twig, twisted, two, type, unable, unassociated, unaware, under, underlain, understand, undone, unfolded, unfortunately, unless, unlikely, unprovable, unrepentant, unsalable, unusual, up, upheaval, upper, uproarious, upward, use, used, valuable, value, valued, variety, vast, vegetation, ventured, vertical, very, viewfinder, vinyl, violating, visible, voices, volunteered, vultures, wait, wake, walking, wall, walls, wandered, want, wanted, war, wares, warn, warriors, was, washing, wasn't, watched, watchful, waterfowl, waterproof, waters, waves, way, ways, we, we've, wealth, weeping, weight, welcome, were, west, wet, whale, what, what's, when, where, whether, which, while, whilst, whiplash, white, Whitehall, whites, whittled, who, whole, wholeheartedly, whose, why, wife, wig, wildlife, will, William, willing, wind, windowsill, wire, wished, wishing, with, without, witnesses, wives, Wm., Wolf, woman, woman's, won't, wonder, wondered, wonderful, wood, words, wore, work, worked, working, workmanship, worth, would, wouldn't, wrested, written, wrong, wrought, year's, years, yelling, yellowed, yet, you, you're, you've, young, zone

PHOTO CREDITS

TEXT CREDITS

Credits and Acknowledgements: pages 9–11, 13–14, 17–18, 133–141, 143–146: Excerpts from *Artifacts*: SOURCE: From Evans, M. (2003). *ARTIFACTS*. Scottsdale, AZ: Poisoned Pen Press. Pages 1–16, 58–60, 98, 284–285. Reprinted with permission; page 41: "Comments from the Classroom" text box reprinted with permission from Alyson Lischka; page 51: excerpt from *Effigies*: SOURCE: From Evans, M. (2007). *EFFIGIES*. Scottsdale, AZ: Poisoned Pen Press. Reprinted with permission; page 67: "One Blogger's Perception of the Beauty of Math" text box reprinted with permission from Brent Yorgey; page 78: "Sir Cumference" text box reprinted with permission from Cindy Neuschwander; page 80: "Fibonacci Numbers in Nature" text box reprinted with permission from Sarah Campbell; page 99: *the curvature of spacetime* poem reprinted by permission of Johnny Masiulewicz; page 99: "Loving Words the Way Zero Loves One" text box reprinted by permission of Lola Haskins.

INDEX